GOD USES ORDINARY MEN

Portraits of Five Extraordinary Lives

by *Margolyn Woods*

Vital Issues Press

Vital Issues Press
P.O. Box 53788
Lafayette, Louisiana 70505

Library of Congress Card Catalog
Number 96-61824
ISBN 1-56384-139-8

Dedication

To all the people in our lives
who took the time to share the
gospel of Jesus Christ.

2 Timothy 2:2

Contents

Acknowledgments

In my efforts to interview the men in this book, I ran into five very busy men with incredible schedules. I am very thankful to each of them for taking time to share what God has done in their lives. Along with these men, I wish to thank all of the following people who helped to bring this book to fruition, either through their prayers or their direction: Steve Arnold, Jim Bramlett, Jeff Coch, Lianna Debee, Carolyn Dixon, Nathan Dunn, Dave Krueger, Ken Levy, Laura Love, Maureen Mac Lellan, Gwen Marolis, Ron Miller, Bonnie Mize, Larry Moody, Jane Park, Kathy Rogers, Bill Spencer, Suzanne Spencer, Greg Stoughton, Jim Torrey, Laura Watts, and Debbie Woska.

Special thanks to my wonderful husband, Roy Woods, who constantly encourages me through his support and prayers.

—Psalm 96:3

Tell of His glory among the nations,
His wondrous deeds among all of the people.

Chapter One

Dr. Bill Bright

8 May 1996

The entourage of four black limousines sped away from the world famous Claridges Hotel, through the winding streets of London, and past the guard gates of Buckingham Palace, where we were ushered into a large, magnificently decorated room. As we took our places, Prince Phillip himself was announced. We rose as he entered the room, and I was humbled to think that my life's work and love for my Lord Jesus Christ would bring me to this room. I couldn't help but think I was a long way from Coweta, Oklahoma.

October 1921

Born 19 October 1921 on a ranch near Coweta, Oklahoma, I was the seventh child in a family of eight children—five boys, two girls and an older brother who died in infancy. We worked hard on the ranch from early morning until late at night. Everybody worked hard in those days, however, and I have fond memories of a wonderful childhood.

I had no God in my life; although I was baptized when I was twelve years old at the local church. Some unfortunate things happened in the life of that little church, and I became "turned off" by church. The only thing that really challenged me spiritually was my precious, saintly mother. I was truly blessed to have a mother who prayed for me every day of my life and who dedicated me to Christ even before I was born. I didn't realize how blessed I was while growing up with her. I thought all moms were like my mom. It wasn't until later, when I looked back through the years that I realized what a godly woman she was. I did believe that women were to be like their mothers and boys were to be like their fathers, and so I tried to emulate my father.

My father was a materialistic entrepreneur. He was active in the cattle and oil business. His father before him had been a pioneer in the oil business of Oklahoma, and so I grew up with a very materialistic point of view. I believed I could do anything I wanted on my own ability.

I was considered a hard worker and a good student, active in high school affairs, sports, drama, and debate. When I went away to college, I had big dreams. I wanted to be student body president and editor of the yearbook, all of which occurred and more because I worked hard and used my God-given talents. But in those days I didn't give Him due credit.

When I graduated from college, I worked with farmers and ranchers as part of the extension faculty at Oklahoma State University. It was a wonderful job; I even had the privilege of training the livestock judging team from Muskogee, Oklahoma, who placed first at the American Royal that year!

They paid me many times what I was worth, but it wasn't enough to suit me. I was ambitious and had big dreams, so I decided to move to California.

The war had begun about this time, and it was a very difficult time in Oklahoma and across America. Many of my family and friends were in the military, but I wasn't accepted because of a perforated eardrum. With the help of my local draft board, I sought to enlist in every branch of the military but to no avail. This was a time when all Americans were patriotic and wanted to do their patriotic duty for their country, and I was no exception. I pulled every string I knew including contacting Harry Truman, who was then Chairman of the Military House Committee, but I was rejected.

I believed my chances to enlist might be better in California, and so I went with the specific purpose of enlisting in one of the branches of the armed services. I ended up working in a shipyard for the war effort.

It didn't work out as I planned, though. I realized early on that, although they were paying us for ten hours of work each day, the money was going to line the pockets of the contractors who worked on a cost plus basis. I threatened to expose them to the *Los Angeles Times,* but they didn't change. They simply tried to buy me off with promotions.

I finally decided to quit and go into business for myself. I chose a very fancy *epicurean* line of brandied foods, called Bright's California Confections. I had the good fortune of meeting two men during this time, who took me under their wings, treated me like a son and helped me with contacts into some of the finest stores across America. These included Neiman Marcus, J.W. Robinsons, and Bullock's Wilshire. I soon had thirty-seven items—fruits, candies, jams, and jellies—all of the highest quality and beautifully packaged.

Time went on and in the course of events, My mother's prayers caught up with me through a series of circumstances. I was enjoying success and even had a live amateur radio program each Sunday, after which I usually went horseback riding in the Hollywood Hills. During this time, I became close to an elderly couple who took a liking to me. Whenever they saw me, they talked about an incredible preacher at Hollywood Presbyterian Church, and they repeatedly invited me to attend with them. Well, their persistence finally got the best of me, and on my way back from the stables one day, I slipped into the back row of the church.

Hollywood "Press" (as it's often called) soon became a big part of my life. I was initially attracted to the wealthy and influential of the church. Many activities were held in their palatial homes. One stands out in particular. A prime developer of the famed Bel Air district opened his home to groups from the church. We swam in his pool, ate his wonderful food, and sat listening to conversations about Jesus Christ. Nurtured by Christian fellowship, I began to study the Bible and to let God influence my life.

It was at one of these occasions that I heard Dr. Henrietta Mears, Director of Christian Education at Hollywood Press, speak about Paul's conversion on the road to Damascus. She shared that Paul was on his way to persecute Christians when he met the living Christ, and God changed his life. She added that Paul responded, saying, "Lord, what will you have me to do?"

Dr. Mears challenged all of us present that evening to ask that same question. That night I got down on my knees in the privacy of my home and asked, "Lord, what will you have me do?" I had received approximately six months thus far of Bible study and preaching, and I recognized that God indeed did have a plan and purpose for my life. I had been introduced to prominent and successful people in the community who were more excited about Jesus Christ than their bank accounts or prestige. This was a revelation to me because until this time, I had always believed that Christianity was pretty much for the down and outers and people who needed a crutch. But, these wealthy, influential people had everything their hearts could desire, and yet they were more excited about Jesus Christ than anything else in their lives. This made quite an impression on me.

All of this led me to conclude that the God of creation Who flung into space at least fifty billion galaxies and Who created man is the one, true living and loving God. He came to planet earth in the person of Jesus of Nazareth, the visible expression of the invisible God. He died on the cross for my sins, was raised from the dead, and now lives at the right hand of the Father interceding for me today. And, simply by asking Him into my life as my Lord and Savior I have the incredible gift of eternal life with Him.

It is still awesome to believe that God, our holy and heavenly Father, would come to earth, die for my sins, and dwell in a sinful person like me. It's hard to believe that we are His children and heirs of God through the gift of His Son, Jesus Christ!

I learned that God speaks to us through His Son, Jesus Christ, whom He appointed heir of all things, and through whom also He made the world (Heb. 1). And, I learned that "He is the image of the invisible God, the first born of all creation. For by Him all things were created both in heaven and on earth, visible, whether thrones or dominions or rulers or authorities—all things have been created by Him and for Him" (Col. 1:15-16).

Jesus loved me enough to die for me, and through His Word and His people, I fell in love with Him, and committed my life to live for Him as my Lord and Savior.

Vonette Zachary Bright

My wife of forty-eight years is from the same small community of 1500 people. Vonette was a city girl, however, and I was a country boy living out on a ranch. I was five years older than she was, so I had no romantic interest in her. Being fond of beauty, however, I certainly noticed her. Vonette was always an outstanding and a beautiful young lady.

It was at the Coconut Grove one evening when I saw Diana Lynn walk by. Vonette came back to my mind, because Diana looked a lot like Vonette, and I turned and asked my sister, "What ever happened to that pretty Vonette Zachary?"

She told me she was attending Texas Women's University, and I wrote her a letter the very next day. I told her I had seen Diana Lynn and that she had reminded me of her. I was just writing to say, "Hello" and to ask how she was doing. Then I wished her a good summer. Before long we were writing each other regularly and then daily!

We finally got together, and after a very short time we fell in love. I proposed, and before we knew it we were planning a wedding. We had a long engagement, however, as I promised Vonette's parents we would wait until Vonette graduated from college to get married.

Yet, there was one thing about Vonette that bothered me—the question of her dedication to the Lord. During our time together, I remember saying that God would have to come first in our marriage. This annoyed her. "I'm not sure that's right," she bristled, "I think a man's family should be his first concern."

The matter of Vonette's personal relationship with Christ continued to trouble me as I transferred from Princeton Theological Seminary to Fuller Theological Seminary in 1947 to be closer to my business, Bright's California Confections.

Nevertheless, I had been so impressed that God had chosen Vonette to be my wife. Although I had dated many girls prior to our engagement, and had been infatuated with some, I had never felt led to propose to any of them. I felt confident even before our first date that Vonette was the one with whom I was to share my life and my ministry for Christ.

This was one of the greatest conflicts of my life! What was I to do? I had committed my life to Christ and to His service, and now I was in love with and engaged to a girl who, although an active church member, was not even a Christian! Obviously, we could not marry if she were not a Christian. Yet, I had been so sure.

Finally, the day of graduation came for Vonette, and she received her degree in home economics from Texas Women's University. I suggested she visit her brother, who lived near me in southern California. She apparently thought this was a good idea, too, a sort of do-or-die time. Later, she told me that she confided in a girlfriend, "I am either going to rescue Bill from this religious fanaticism or come home without a ring!" She did neither.

While in California, Vonette went with me to a meeting of several hundred students at Forest Home, the famous conference center for Christian leadership established by Dr. Mears. Even though I had introduced many people to Jesus Christ, I did not know how to reach Vonette. Someone else would have to help me, and Dr. Mears was the logical choice. She had counseled with thousands of young people and knew how to communicate with individuals who had inquiring and scientific minds.

By this time, Vonette had begun to doubt the Bible and even the existence of God. I felt she needed help from someone who knew more than I did. Also, because of our emotional involvement, I was afraid that I might be able to get a verbal commitment to Christ, but not a commitment of her will. She might say, "yes" to Christ with her lips in order to please me and not mean it in her heart.

While Dr. Mears and Vonette talked, I paced back and forth outside the cottage, praying. Time dragged on—fifteen minutes, an hour, and more! Suddenly, the door burst open and Vonette came bounding out into my arms. There were tears of joy on her cheeks and an indescribable look of radiance on her face. She didn't need to say a word. I knew what had happened, and tears of gratitude filled my eyes, too. The wedding date was set, and we were married on 30 December 1948.

Vonette and I became increasingly convinced that living for and serving Christ was our major goal in life. As a result of this awareness, we decided we would sign a contract with the Lord. No one had suggested this; it was just something we decided to do together. I had signed many contracts as a businessman, so it made sense that we should sign a contract with the most important person in our lives. Both of us had been very materialistic and self-centered prior to becoming Christians, and now the Lord had replaced this selfishness with a desire to serve Him. So, on a Sunday afternoon, Vonette went into one room in our Hollywood Hills home, and I went into another while we made lists of all the things we wanted in our lives. When I had first proposed to Vonette, we had talked about a honeymoon in Europe, about securing the finest voice teacher to develop her beautiful singing voice, and about living in a fabulous home in Bel-Air. Now, all of this was secondary; our new lists were surprisingly similar:

1. To live holy lives, controlled and empowered by the Holy Spirit.
2. To be effective witnesses for Christ.
3. To help fulfill the Great Commission in our generation.

We also wanted a Christian home with two to four children. (We now have two sons.) We also thought it would be convenient to have two cars. (Today we don't own any, but God has provided us transportation through the generosity of a friend who is also interested in helping to reach the world for Christ.) Finally, if the Lord would be pleased, we wanted a home nice enough to invite the President of the United States and modest enough that a man from skid row would feel comfortable.

We signed our names to these lists as a formal act of commitment to Christ and His cause. This was an especially significant commitment inasmuch as we were doing it together as a young husband and wife. There was no particular emotion involved; it was simply a transaction of our united wills. What was to happen as a result of this commitment we did not know; but as we continued our studies, our teaching ministry, deputation work and business, His plan began to unfold.

One evening at about midnight during my senior year in seminary, I was studying for a final exam. There was nothing unusual about the setting or about the circumstances. Vonette was asleep in a nearby room. Suddenly, without warning or without any indication of what was going to happen, I sensed the presence of God in a way I had never before known. Although it could not have lasted more than a few seconds, I suddenly had the overwhelming impression that the Lord had flashed on the screen of my mind His instructions for my life and ministry.

It is difficult to talk about such experiences for fear of being misunderstood or causing others to seek similar experiences; but I think I know a little something of what the Apostle Paul experienced when he met the Lord in such a dramatic way on the road to Damascus. In any event, this was the greatest spiritual experience of my Christian life! At this time and in a very definite way, God commanded me to invest my life in helping to fulfill the Great Commission in this generation. I was to begin by helping to win and disciple students of the world for Christ. How to do this was not spelled out in detail; that came later as the Lord gave me insights and direction. I awakened Vonette, and together we praised God for His direction and promised that with His grace and strength we would obey Him.

The following day I went to one of my favorite seminary professors, Dr. Wilbur Smith, and told him what God had revealed to me. He immediately shared my enthusiasm, and the next morning he called me out of his classroom and handed me a piece of paper on which he had scribbled three letters—CCC. He explained that God had provided a name for my vision—Campus Crusade for Christ. The name stuck.

Since that spring midnight experience, it has been my passion and concern to be obedient to the heavenly vision which God gave me that night.

UCLA 1951

After five years of theological graduate study and running my business, I left seminary before graduating. Although I have a great respect and appreciation for the clergy, I believed that my layman status would help me in the ministry to which I felt called. So, I left seminary, sold my fancy foods business, and moved with Vonette to a rental house one block from the campus of UCLA. We began by holding meetings in our home, which was adjacent to sorority row. Within a short time, hundreds of students were attending. My goal at first was to reach some of the influential campus leaders. This was accomplished when both the student body president and the editor of the campus newspaper gave their lives to

Christ along with Rafer Johnson, world decathlon champion at that time!

Word traveled quickly, and soon we were being asked to begin similar outreach programs on different campuses. As a result, we recruited our first full-time staff, and by the fall of 1952 Campus Crusade for Christ had been established at the University of Washington, the University of California at Berkeley, the University of Southern California, and San Diego State University. By 1960 Campus Crusade for Christ had spread to forty different campuses and to two foreign countries!

As Campus Crusade for Christ grew, I wrote a twenty minute presentation of God's plan which proved to be extremely effective. We soon realized, however, that we needed a much shorter version of the gospel in order to communicate quickly, clearly, and simply to those whose hearts were already open to receiving Christ. I prepared a condensed outline of God's plan, complete with Scripture verses and diagrams, and asked the staff to memorize it. For several years, we wrote it out as we were sharing Christ in witnessing experiences. Then as more and more people became involved in the training program of Campus Crusade, it became apparent that we needed to make our presentation available in printed form to ensure faithfulness to the content and uniformity of the presentation. Thus, the Four Spiritual Laws booklet was born.

As the name suggests, there are four basic truths that all men should know.

The Four Spiritual Laws:

1. God loves you and offers a wonderful plan for your life.

2. Man is sinful and separated from God, thus he cannot know and experience God's love and plan for his life.

3. Jesus Christ is God's provision for man's sin. Through Him you can know and experience God's love and plan for your life.

4. We must individually receive Jesus Christ as Savior and Lord; then we can know and experience God's love and plan for our lives.

This little booklet is so simple that one marvels at its effectiveness. I could tell you hundreds of thrilling stories of how God has used this booklet to reach people who had not responded to previous presentations. There is no magic in the Four Spiritual Laws booklet. I believe God blesses its use because it contains the essence of the gospel, especially when it is used by men and women who are controlled and empowered by the Holy Spirit.

Campus Crusade for Christ

The ministry of Campus Crusade spread beyond campuses to other segments of society. In Dallas at EXPLO 72, eighty thousand people were trained in discipleship and evangelism at a weeklong convention. The international outreach expanded. At EXPLO 74 in Korea, 323,000 were trained in discipleship and evangelism and returned to communities to witness for our Lord. One evening I spoke on the importance of faith for salvation, and approximately one million people indicated their desire to receive Christ as their Savior and Lord!

HERE'S LIFE KOREA in 1980 drew some of the largest crowds in history for any kind of meeting—from two to three million people present each night! And EXPLO 85 was the largest Christian satellite conference ever, linking ninety-five nations to train almost 300,000 Christians to become Christian leaders for our Lord!

Today Campus Crusade operates on a thousand campuses and in 165 different countries. God also opened the door for fifteen other ministries through Campus Crusade, including an inner city ministry (Here's Life, Inner City), a ministry to our politicians (Christian Embassy), a ministry to marriages (Family Life Ministry), Josh McDowell ministries, Executive Ministries, Athletes in Action, and *Challenge Magazine*, just to name a few.

Among the most ambitious of Campus Crusade for Christ's efforts has been *The Jesus Film*, the biblical story of Christ according to the Gospel of Luke. This film includes a cast of 5,000 and has been seen by an estimated 800 million people in 217 countries, and in 375 languages.

God has graciously used this boy from Coweta, Oklahoma, simply because he made himself available to Him. God says He is no respecter of persons. He just needs us to give ourselves over to Him to be used by Him. I could never have imagined the joy and fulfillment that I would receive just by simply living my life as a slave to our blessed Lord.

My God-given goal has been to *help* take the gospel to everybody on the planet by the end of the year 2000. I have tried to be obedient to that heavenly vision now for forty-five years, and, God willing, I shall spend the rest of my life in service to Him and this cause; for Jesus may be coming back soon for His people. I want to be ready to meet Him with at least one billion new believers whom we have helped to introduce to our dear Savior.

8 May 1996

Prince Phillip stood regally in front of me as he awarded me the Templeton Prize for Progress in Religion—previously an award presented to such notables as Mother Theresa, Charles Colson,

Aleksandr Solzhenitsyn, and Billy Graham. He handed me a beautiful silver medal plus a check for $1,057,910.00!!

In humble gratitude I remarked, "I accept this prize in the name of our wonderful Lord and Savior, Jesus Christ, Whom I have sought to serve for more than fifty years."

"What are you going to do with all of this money?" asked Prince Phillip at the end of the presentation.

"Every penny will go to reaching the world for Christ. Through literature, seminars, radio, film, and television, I trust that we shall help to encourage and equip millions of Christians around the world to join us in fasting and praying for world revival and for the fulfillment of our Lord's great commission," I responded.

Even though I could momentarily call myself a millionaire, I could think of no better way to spend the money than to promote revival and fulfillment of the great commission by stirring the hearts of millions of believers to be more faithful in their walk and witness for Christ according to 1 John 2:1-6.

My little children, I am telling you this so that you will stay away from sin. But if you sin, there is someone to plead for you before the Father. His name is Jesus Christ, the one who is all that is good and who pleases God completely. He is the one who took God's wrath against our sins upon himself, and brought us into fellowship with God; and he is the forgiveness for our sins, and not only ours but all the world's.

And how can we be sure that we belong to him? By looking within ourselves: are we really trying to do what he wants us to?

Someone may say, "I am a Christian; I am on my way to heaven; I belong to Christ." But if he doesn't do what Christ tells him to, he is a liar. But those who do what Christ tells them to will learn to love God more and more. That is the way to know whether or not you are a Christian. Anyone who says he is a Christian should live as Christ did. (*The Living Bible*)

Following this magnificent and memorable occasion, we once again entered our limousines and made our way across the palace courtyard heading back to the hotel.

Returning to Claridges Hotel, I found myself thanking the Lord for this incredible honor. As we sat at an elegant luncheon hosted by Sir John Templeton (originator of the prized award), his son, and different lords and ladies of honor, I was reminded that the Lord had bestowed this honor upon Vonette and me because of the contract we had signed back in 1951 dedicating ourselves to being slaves of Jesus Christ.

This award truly belonged to Vonette, too. Though God originally gave me the vision, Vonette concurred and has been a great partner and helper. I refer to her as the co-founder of Campus Crusade for Christ. She has had her own ministry within the organization from its inception, and she was truly one of the prayer warriors who kept this ministry undergirded with prayer.

Through the years, many honors, applause, and praises have come to me, but the greatest privilege and honor I have had is being a slave to Jesus Christ and knowing that one day the greatest prize of all will come. I trust and I pray I'll be worthy of Him saying, "Well, done, my good and faithful servant."

Oftentimes, I am given credit for the phenomenal ministry of Campus Crusade—credit which I do not deserve or seek. The real credit must go to the Lord, because in His sovereign wisdom and grace, He has called a most unusually gifted group of men and women to assist me in the direction and leadership of the ministry.

I'm very humbled by the Templeton Prize, and I don't minimize it. But, it seems so incongruent that this slave of Jesus has received one of the most prestigious awards man can receive. I see this prize as simply something else to lay on the altar as an expression of my love and gratitude to Him.

In closing, I urge all in reach of this message to join with me in humbling ourselves before our almighty, loving, and holy God. Let us fast and pray, seek His face, and ask Him for a great, worldwide spiritual awakening. Please, join with me and millions of other believers in the most exciting, incredibly fulfilling, richly rewarding experiences the human spirit can ever know—to help fulfill the Great Commission of our Lord, sharing God's love and forgiveness with every person on planet Earth.

UREUS

Chapter Two

Larry Mize

I was born in Augusta, Georgia, and that provides part of the reason that I'm so fond of that famous golf tournament in Augusta. I was very fortunate to grow up with loving parents, a brother six years older, and a sister three years older. My parents took us to church, and I learned about Jesus Christ and the Bible at an early age and believed it to be true. I even went forward in a service and accepted Christ and was baptized later in that church. (As it turned out, I didn't really understand what I was doing. I probably did it just because I felt it was the thing to do.)

I fell in love with the game of golf at an early age. My Dad took up the game when I was seven years old and took me along with him. We even went out and watched the Masters Tournament together. I remember anxiously awaiting to turn thirteen because that was the minimum age to work at Augusta National during the tournament! Fortunately, I was assigned the scoreboard on the third hole of the front nine, so I was able to watch the field on the back nine when they had passed me.

Recently, while I was playing the Southern Open, my parents came over to watch and brought me the little pin with the word "Employee" on it from the 1973 Masters Tournament. It was a simple reminder of how much I really love the game of golf! I can't ever remember wanting to do anything else. My middle son, Patrick, who is only seven and a half years old, wants to be a baseball player when he grows up. I'm not sure how he'll do that, but I *always* wanted to be a golfer. So, it's a dream come true that I'm playing golf for a living.

I continued to play golf through high school and college at Georgia Tech, where I majored in Industrial Management. Golf was the most important thing in my life. It was the only thing I wanted to do. I wanted to be just like Jack Nicklaus and get all of the fame and fortune that goes with a successful (Professional Golf Association) career!

After Georgia Tech I went on to the PGA tour school. Most of you may know that the tour school is actually a series of qualifying tournaments. It's not really a school at all. If it were a school, I probably wouldn't be writing this. When I did qualify, there were two rounds of tournaments. First, there were local tournaments in about five or six different spots around the country. Then, twenty or so players advanced to the finals. Today, they go through a three-stage process where the locals are in about five or six regions around the country. Then there are five or six sectionals after which twenty or so players advance to the finals. At the finals today, I think they give away forty tour cards. So, it's really a system where you just play your way onto the tour.

Well, finally, on my third try in the fall of 1981, I did earn my tour card. I got in by the skin of my teeth, and in January of 1982, I started my first year on the tour. I knew I had to make the top 125 money-winners on the official money list to keep my card. It's changed a lot since then; you only had to make $28,000 to keep your card then versus $150,000 or so now. (The purses have really gone up.) By August of that year, I had made a whopping $6,000! (The sports section of the newspaper wasn't even big enough to show where I was on the money list.)

In May 1982, I asked my high school sweetheart to marry me. Bonnie and I had dated since she was in the ninth grade, and I was in the tenth. We dated until our senior year when my Dad, who worked for Southern Bell, was transferred to Augusta, Georgia. I think both of us went out with someone else once during that year. Then, I went to Georgia Tech and she went to the University of Georgia in Athens, Georgia. For a date, we would both drive half way to the Mc Donalds (about thirty miles each) I will never forget asking for Bonnie's hand in marriage. Her father was on a fishing trip, so I went to her mother to ask if I could marry her daughter. I was very nervous, looking at the floor and shuffling my feet. Whether I got around to asking or not, I'm not sure, but her mother said, "Yes," and I got out of there.

We were married in August 1982. Bonnie later told me that her father wasn't so sure it was a good idea to marry me since I didn't have any money and was struggling on the PGA tour. Fortunately, he liked me and allowed her to marry me. The companionship, support, and encouragement she gives me have been invaluable.

I'll never forget the next tournament at Hartford. I wanted to prove to everybody that I had made the right decision by getting married. I shot twelve under; I was pretty excited. But, as you may remember, we used to play the Hartford Tournament at Weathersfield where everybody shot really low. I think Tim Norris shot twenty-five under! I shot twelve under and made $1,700, which wasn't a whole lot.

My play improved as that year went along. At the last tournament, the Disney World Classic, I found myself in good position after three days. On the weekend, I "birdied" holes 15, 16, and 17 and made par on 18 to finish thirteen under par. My money list position improved from 152nd to 124th. This secured my exemption for the following year. I was ecstatic!

In June 1983 I was paired with "Fuzzy" Zoeller and "Chip" Beck at the Danny Thomas Memphis Classic. I came to the last hole tied for the lead with Chip, Fuzzy, and Sammy Rachels. Chip missed his chip shot, and I had about a twenty-five footer for birdie. I still have bruises on the inside of my knees where they were shaking over that putt, but I knocked the putt into the hole. Fuzzy hit a great putt but missed; I had won my first tournament. Here I was twenty-four years old, and I had just won my first tournament. I was on cloud nine. Things were great.

We were now able to move out of my parents' home and get our own place just a mile down the road. You know, as a child I thought golf was going to give me everything I needed, and right now it looked like things were well on their way.

I didn't win a tournament in 1984 even though I continued to play better. Actually, I think I finished one spot lower on the money list even though I made more money because the purses continued to increase.

In 1985 I continued to play well and finished even higher on the money list. I didn't win again, but I was building my confidence and trying to become a better player. Then in 1986, I played at the Players Championship in Jacksonville, Florida. Other than the four Majors—The Masters, The U.S. Open, The British Open, and The PGA—this is probably the biggest tournament in the world and maybe has the strongest field in the world. I shot 66, 68, and 66 and was just playing phenomenally. I was sixteen under par with a four-shot lead and people thought, "Larry will win this tournament, and he will finally get back in the winner's circle."

With four holes to play, I had a three-shot lead. By the end of the match, I lost by one. This was a devastating loss for me because golf was my life. Bonnie was eight months pregnant at the time, and I was not exactly easy to live with that next week at home. It was during this week that Bonnie and I attended our first Tour Bible Study. It was really a wonderful experience for both of us, and Wednesday nights became our time for Bible Study and fellowship because I hoped to be playing golf on Sundays—required in tournament play.

I traveled alone to the Masters as Bonnie was too far along to go with me and had to stay home. I had a good last round and finished sixteenth, which was always good at Augusta because the top twenty-four get invited back to play the next year. Everyone wants to win a golf tournament, but if you don't win, you want to make sure you finish in the top twenty-four so you can come back.

I went right from the Masters to the Heritage Classic at Harbour Town at Hilton Head, South Carolina. This is one of my favorite golf courses. At registration that afternoon, a security guard came up to me and told me to call my wife. I panicked, but the guard told me that everything was fine. She was already dilating and things were speeding along. As I was only five hours from home, I withdrew from the tournament and drove home to be with her. In the morning, I rejoined my wife for the delivery and witnessed a miracle; the birth of our first son, David!

Later that afternoon, as Bonnie rested, I held David in my arms and looked into his tiny face. God had given me an instant love for this baby, and it dawned on me that God was trying to get my attention through the miracle of birth. It was as if He spoke to me. I knew that the birth of a child—both the conception and even the formation in the womb—could only be from God.

It was as if God were saying, "Larry, did you see this miracle that just happened? I now need you to be the father and husband that I want you to be." He made it so clear that I was being entrusted with invaluable privileges and awesome responsibilities.

I realized that I needed to get my act together. I had always believed in God with my head, but I had never trusted Him with my life.

Golf had been my life. It's how I make my living, but I now knew that I needed to put my faith and trust in Jesus Christ, and so in that hospital room I turned my life over to Him. I had always put Jesus Christ in the "back seat of my car" as a passenger, but now I wanted Him in the "front seat" driving in my life!

I'd like to tell a story that really describes the transformation that happened to me that day. Blondin, the famous nineteenth century French tightrope walker, successfully crossed Niagara Falls a number of times. It's an 1100 foot span, 160 feet above the raging waters. On one occasion, he pushed a wheelbarrow across. He then asked how many in the crowd believed he could push the wheelbarrow across with someone in it. The crowd cheered.

He then asked, "Does anyone believe in me enough to get into the wheelbarrow and cross Niagara Falls with me." No one volunteered.

Finally, Blondin's manager climbed on his back, and they crossed the great falls together. The crowd's belief was purely intellectual, which is what my belief in Jesus Christ was prior to this time. Blondin's manager went beyond intellectual belief to personal trust. This is the kind of faith the Bible says we must have in Christ.

I thought I had done what I was supposed to do when I accepted Jesus Christ as a child, but I didn't really understand what I was doing. I only accepted Him intellectually, I believed He was Who He said He was, and that was as far as it went. I never accepted His sacrifice for my own sins.

That day in the hospital, I decided to put my faith and my life into His hands.

John 3:16 says, "For God so loved the world that He gave his only begotten Son, that whoever believes in Him should not perish but have eternal life." Verse 17 goes on and says, "For God did not send

His Son into the world to judge the world but that the world should be saved through Him." We have a loving God.

For the first time I understood that I was separated from God because of my sins. God cannot accept even a little bit of sin because it's like putting one drop of cyanide in a glass of water. It poisons the entire glass. I wouldn't drink it, and neither would you. In the same way, God cannot allow even a small amount of sin into heaven lest it would contaminate the entire place. Romans 3:23 says, "For all have sinned and fallen short of the glory of God." But, God loves all of us so much that He sent His Son, Jesus Christ, God in the flesh, to walk this earth, and die a horrible, humiliating death on the cross as payment for our sins. The Son of God then rose from the dead on the third day to give us eternal life with God. 1 Peter 3:18 says, "For Christ died for sins once for all, the righteous, for the unrighteous, to bring you to God. He was put to death in the body but made alive by the Spirit." 1 John 4:10 says, "In this love, not that we love God, but that He loved us and sent His Son to be propitiation [satisfactory payment] for our sins." To me, this is the ultimate love story.

I thought being a professional golfer and gaining fame and fortune were going to provide me with everything I needed. I found out it didn't. There's a void in all of us, and I had tried to fill that void with the fame and fortune of being a "pro" golfer. I made lots of money, I won tournaments, and I had a great wife, but it was never enough. Something was always missing, and that something was Jesus Christ. Receiving Christ filled that void and gave me a peace and joy that go beyond my understanding. Philippians 4:6-7 says, "Be anxious for nothing, but in everything by prayer and supplication with thanksgiving let your requests be made known to God. And the peace of God, which surpasses all comprehension, shall guard your hearts and minds in Christ Jesus."

You know, all of a sudden, I didn't necessarily play better, but I had an underlying peace and joy. I wasn't always happy, but I felt the security that God loved me and that He'd never leave me.

I had another good year in 1986 and finished high on the money list again. And then in 1987, I decided to play again in that little tournament in Augusta with big names like Crenshaw, Maltbie, Norman, Ballesteros, Langer, and Strange. I was hoping I could just slip in unnoticed and maybe win the tournament. Sure enough, with nine holes to play, I was just one shot out of the lead. I saw my name on the leaderboard walking off the tenth tee, and I told myself not to look at the leaderboard because it made me nervous. After a couple of birdies at the twelfth and thirteenth holes, I was leading by one shot and then bogeyed the fourteenth and fifteenth. Now I was trailing by one shot. After pars on holes sixteen and seventeen, I needed to birdie the tough finishing hole. It was a big moment for me when I birdied hole eighteen. I finished three under par for the tournament. Now, all I could do was wait to see if that score would be good enough to win the tournament. Steve Ballesteros finished at three under par as did Greg Norman, who had just narrowly missed a birdie on the final hole. So, the three of us had to have a playoff.

Even though I was the underdog, I had a lot of confidence going into the play-off because I had played so well all week and that birdie on the last hole was a tremendous boost. On the first hole, hole number ten, Ballesteros surprisingly bogeyed, leaving Norman and me to go on to the next hole. We both hit the fairway, but my second shot, a five iron, went way right of the green. Norman hit his second shot on the right fringe of the green about fifty feet away. I was faced with a 140 foot chip shot. I wanted to put the shot somewhere around the hole to put the pressure on Norman because his long putt wasn't easy to make in two putts. I hit an aggressive "bump and run" shot that landed short of the green because the green was too hard to land the ball on it directly. Incredibly, I had the right line, and the ball found the bottom of the cup to win the Masters Tournament! This was the thrill of a lifetime, especially for a boy who grew up right there in Augusta.

People often ask, "What were you thinking about then?"

I reply, "I think my running, jumping, and screaming probably say it all." I was also thinking about being able to come back to the Masters every year, because winning gives you a lifetime invitation.

Obviously this win was a great thrill, but the most exciting thing was that it gave me an opportunity to share my faith. All of a sudden, people wanted to hear what a Masters champion had to say. I wanted to let people know that you can be successful in this world, you can be competitive in this world, and you can be a winner in this world, yet you can still have a personal relationship with Jesus Christ.

Prior to 1986 I wanted to play for me, I wanted the glory. It was me, me, me. Since that day when my first son was born, I have wanted to give all the glory to God. As it says in 1 Corinthians 10:31, "Whether, then, you eat or drink or whatever you do, do all to the glory of God."

I can never do anything to repay God for what He's done for me. It's a free gift that I gladly accept through Jesus Christ.

Ephesians 2:8-9 says, "For by grace you have been saved through faith; and that not of yourselves, it is the gift of God; not as a result of works, that no one should boast." The one thing I want to do is glorify God in whatever I do. When I win golf tournaments, I want to glorify and praise Him, not just for the win, but for what He has done in my life. He has given me eternal life through Jesus Christ and a sense of love, joy, and peace that can only come from God.

After the Masters I had a great year. Everybody talks about the Grand Slam but that's really no big deal. (Ha! ha!) I talk about the Georgia Slam, because there are three tournaments in Georgia. There are The Masters, The Atlantia Classic, and The Buick Challenge which is held near Columbus. I figured if I could win the Georgia Slam; you know, Bobby Jones and Jack Nicklaus move over. (Ha! again.)

I finished second at Atlanta and second at the Buick Challenge, even though

I finished four shots back each time. It was a distant second, but it still made it a really a great year for me.

I went on that year and made enough points to be on the Ryder Cup team. It's one of the greatest experiences and honors that any American or European golfer can have. The competition is like no other tournament in that a team of American golfers competes against a team of European golfers. The camaraderie each team has is wonderful. When we're not playing, we're out there on the golf course cheering each other on to victory. We get together and have meetings, and it's just a tremendous thrill to play on the team.

After that year, some people said, "Well, Larry is really going to take off now. You know, he'll kind of come into his own, and everything will be great."

In 1988 and 1989, for the first time in my career, my play got worse rather than better. I finished sixty-second and forty-fifth on the money list. I thought this was horrible. I was really frustrated and my anger was coming back. I thought I had to live up to being a Masters Champion. I wasn't supposed to play badly!

I actually thought about doing something else for a living. (I now laugh as I think back on that thought.) In May of 1989 I called Larry Moody, our Tour Bible Study leader and president of Search Ministries out of Ellicott City, Maryland. I told him of my struggles and frustrations, and he helped me to realize that I was trying to get my significance from golf and being a Masters Champion. He reminded me that I am significant for one reason and one reason only; because God loves me enough to send His Son, Jesus Christ, as payment for my sins. God wants me to have a personal relationship with Him through Jesus Christ. Winning the Masters and anything else I do in my golf career is great, but my significance as well as my security and satisfaction are in Jesus Christ.

Larry challenged me to spend more time studying the Bible. He said that the Bible was the key to learning how God wanted me to live my life. My relationship with God started back when I made that decision in 1986, but I needed to look to God and God's Word for direction in my life daily.

I cried as I hung up the phone that day and I felt God's cleansing as I released my struggles.

I played the rest of that year with a lot more peace and joy than I'd ever had previously. The year 1990 came along and I didn't win any golf tournaments, but I finished as high as I ever had without winning a golf tournament. I finished fourteenth on the money list.

At the end of the year, I went to Japan for the Dunlop Phoenix Tournament. I had been fortunate enough to win this tournament in 1989, so I was defending my title, and praise God, I won it again!

As I mentioned, I like to give God the praise and glory when I win, but as I got to the press room that day, I thought, "I'm in Japan and Christianity isn't very big over here, maybe I shouldn't say anything."

But, then I thought about John 12:43. (Larry Moody had been leading a study in the book of John.) The Scripture talks about the Pharisees. They believed in Jesus, but they weren't confessing Him lest they be put out of the synagogue. In verse forty-three it says, "For they loved the approval of men rather than the approval of God."

This truth really hit me; I was worried what the Japanese were going to think and not what God would think. I said a quiet little prayer right then and asked for guidance and for God to give me the strength to do what was right.

A couple of minutes later when there was a lull in the questions I turned to Nicki, my interpreter, and said, "Nicki, I would like to do one thing. I would like to give God the glory and thank Him for what He's done for me through Jesus Christ."

As she repeated what I said in Japanese, I saw many of the reporters busy writing. I don't know what everybody thought, but I wasn't concerned because I knew I was doing what God wanted.

The following week I played at the Casio World Open in Japan. They play the Pro-Ams a little differently over there. Here we play eighteen holes, and you may or you may not go eat with your group afterwards. In Japan you play nine holes, eat lunch with your group, and then play the back nine. It's a tradition over there.

Normally, there isn't much conversation during lunch, just a lot of nodding and smiling. But, this day one of the Japanese men turned to me and said in English, "I hear you are a Christian and read the Bible."

I said, "Yes, I do." As we carried on a conversation, I marveled at how God was able to use me wherever I happened to be as long as I was faithful to Him.

In 1991 and 1992 I didn't play as well as I would have liked, but I worked hard on my swing and it paid off the following year.

In 1993 I got off to a good start by playing well in the Tucson Open. After three rounds I was in third place—three shots out of first place. Bonnie and our two boys were flying to Phoenix on Sunday for the following two tournaments. Bonnie had said that she might drive down to Tucson to see me finish, and then we could drive back to Phoenix together. I didn't think they would drive down after the long flight from Georgia, as Bonnie was pregnant with our third child and I knew she would be tired. I putted out for the win on the eighteenth hole, and out of the crowd David and Patrick came running onto the green! I was shocked and it was a wonderful surprise to have my family there to help me celebrate. After the interviews, we drove to the nearest Pizza Hut for dinner.

This was a big win for me as I hadn't won in the United States since the Masters in 1987. It took the proverbial "monkey" off my back.

Later on in 1993, I won the Buick Open and I was back in the Winner's Circle. I had never won two tournaments in one year, and it was a thrill. Bonnie and the kids joined me, and afterwards we drove together to the PGA in Toledo, Ohio. This time we traveled with Robert, our newest addition.

There was a lot of traffic on the road that night. The boys had fallen asleep in the back of the car, and I remember Bonnie and I were enjoying some quiet time together.

"Bonnie," I said, "this is really great. I've never won two tournaments in one year before, and I am really enjoying this."

"But," I added, "it pales in comparison to knowing Jesus Christ as my Lord and Savior, because as good as the victories are, they don't give me the kind of security, significance, and satisfaction that I get from knowing I have a loving Father who's going to take care of me and who will always be there for me." It was really a neat time of sharing and I really thank God for the truths He's shown me.

Later that year, I got a last minute invitation to the Johnny Walker Tournament. For some reason Greg Norman couldn't play, and the committee had to pick somebody. Since I had played well, they decided to pick me. I went to the tournament thinking, "Well, this is a bonus, even last place is a pretty good check. I'm just going to have a good time here and relax."

I wanted to win, but I hadn't really prepared for the tournament because I didn't know I would be playing. Surprisingly, I played really well and had a three-shot lead going into the last day. I was pretty nervous. As I watched TV in my hotel room Saturday night, I have to admit that the $550,000 first place prize money kept flashing into my head. I thought, "Larry, the money is not why you want to win this thing. Forget about the money." But that's a lot of money!

I got up Sunday morning and a thought struck me. This was going to be Robert's first Christmas. After this tournament, I was going home to have a great Christmas with my family and celebrate the birth of Jesus Christ. I had to give this tournament over to God. All I had to do was give it my best, and that's all I can do. Don't get me wrong, I knew I'd be upset if I didn't play well, but I also knew deep down inside that I was going home to have a great Christmas with my family, and that was the perspective that gave me peace.

Sure enough, I went out there and got off to a good start. After four holes I had a seven-shot lead, "my foot was glued to the pedal," and I wasn't going to let up. I won by ten shots, and it was a great way to end the year, but more importantly, I had my priorities in order—God, family, career.

As the kids get older, they're not able to travel with me as much as I'd like, but I now play a somewhat limited schedule each year, preferring to keep a large measure of my focus on my family. I am currently coaching David's soccer team, and I'm an assistant baseball coach for Patrick.

When I was struggling in 1988 and 1989, I read 1 Peter 1:23-24, and it really meant a lot to me. It says, "For all flesh is like grass and all its glory like the flower of grass. The grass withers, and the flower falls off, but the Word of the Lord abides forever."

I know that's true for me. No matter what I try to do in golf, it's never going to be enough. There's always going to be something more, but my relationship with Jesus Christ is enough. He satisfies me completely, and I am content. He'll never leave me and He'll never forsake me. That's the security and significance that I can get from nothing else, only from a loving Father who created me and wants the best for me.

In closing, I'd just like to share my favorite Scripture. It's Philippians 3:13-

14. Paul is trying to understand the power of Jesus Christ's resurrection. He says, "Brethren, I do not regard myself as having laid hold of it yet; but one thing I do: forgetting what lies behind and reaching forward to what lies ahead, I press on toward the goal for the prize of the upward call of God in Christ Jesus."

That's my goal. I'm not perfect; I make mistakes, and I still sin. But, I keep pressing on because I know there's a God Who forgives me when I confess my sins to Him, and I know he loves me no matter what. I'm going to keep pressing on towards the true goal, the true prize that no golf game can ever match. It's the prize of eternal life with Him.

As a kid, I thought golf was going to get me everything I wanted. I got fame and fortune in the golfing world, and it wasn't enough. But, as soon as I gave Jesus Christ charge of my life, it was enough. He took care of everything. He gave me a peace and joy that I don't understand and a security that God loves me no matter what. He gave His life for me and that makes me pretty significant.

Nothing I did on my own and nothing I can ever do will change His love for me.

Many people ask, "Well, that sounds good, but what do I have to do?"

It's so simple. Jesus tells us that He stands at the door and knocks to come into our lives. What we have to realize is that the door knob to open the door is on our side of the door!

I don't know where you are spiritually, but if you don't know Jesus Christ as your personal Savior, I'd like to share a prayer you can pray to accept Him. Please pray it now, making the words your own.

> Dear God, I admit that I am a sinner, and I understand that my sin separates me from you. I believe that Jesus, being God, paid the penalty for all of my sins when He died on the cross and rose from the dead. I place my trust in You as my personal Savior. Thank you for loving and forgiving me and for giving to me the gift of eternal life. In Jesus' name. Amen.

Receiving Jesus Christ and personally trusting Him for salvation was and is the most important thing in my life. I just ask you to check into it for yourself. It's too important a decision to delay it.

Chapter Three

Cal Thomas

I started in radio when I was only sixteen years old, about two weeks after my voice changed. I joined NBC News in Washington as a copy boy back when we had copy to carry and gender-distinctive positions were not politically incorrect. I decided very early I wanted to be a network television correspondent, and I bent every resource and pursued every avenue to fulfill that objective—not a bad objective, not a bad goal, and not an unworthy business. And yet, the reason for this goal was that I believed once I had achieved my goal, once I had achieved recognition, fame, position, and a certain amount of power, I would be accepted by people. I would even be loved by people, and more importantly, I would validate something within myself of value, worth, and meaning for being alive.

I was taken to the White House to meet my first president by Sander Vanocur, who was then the White House correspondent for NBC News. I met John F. Kennedy and saw a number of people I recognized. Forrest Gump was over in the corner. It was very exciting standing in the White House as a young man meeting famous politicians and the important journalists of our time. I knew I wanted to make a career out of journalism, and I set out on a twelve year game plan to achieve that goal. I thought with enough hard work, dedication, drive, talent, and commitment I would be able to achieve this goal in twelve years! I had an educational game plan, a career game plan, and an economic game plan, and every year on my birthday, I would sit down and examine the previous twelve months and see if I had achieved all of the goals I had set at the beginning of the year. Usually I had not only achieved them, I had surpassed them.

I moved to Houston to get some additional on-air experience in order to come back to Washington. Then at the age of twenty-seven, I became one of the youngest men on the NBC radio and television networks.

"NBC Radio news on the hour brought to you by Di-Gel." I see you all remember those days. Fortunately, this was just before they started advertising Preparation H on the radio. I never had to say those words, I'm happy to say.

I began to do all of the things that people say you should do when you begin to gain position, power, and money. I went to the fancy parties and hung around the famous people. I began to buy stuff. I bought the fancy clothes, new car, and the nice house in the suburbs. My vision and view of myself was determined largely by what I had and whom I knew. This is the way Washington plays the power game.

By the way, you know what the American Dream is, don't you? Let me summarize it for you: You come home from school one day, you've had a bad day, and you say to your parents, or your day care worker, significant other, guardian, or whatever, "Gee, I've had a terrible day at school, I think I'll quit."

And, your parents say, "Well, Honey, you can't quit."

And, you say, "Well, why not?"

"Well, you have to get a good education."

"Why do I need a good education?"

"So you can get a good job."

"Why do I need a good job?"

"So you can make money."

"Why?"

"So you can buy things?"

"Why?"

"So you'll be happy."

Now, summarized and boiled down, isn't this basically the American Dream? Get a good education so you can get a good job, so you can make money, so you can buy things, so you'll be happy.

I've never met anyone who said, "You know, this job I have is just perfect for me. I don't need a promotion."

Or, "I love what I do, I can't ever imagine doing anything else in my life."

Or, "The salary I'm making is perfectly adequate for all of my needs. I don't need a raise, I'm in good shape."

Or, "This car I'm driving is a great car. I'm going to keep it forever. I'll never trade it in on a new model."

Or, "The house I'm living in is perfectly adequate for my needs. I don't need a bigger or better house."

We're constantly aspiring for greater and supposedly better things. Has anyone ever arrived at the state of contentment and peace by the accumulation of material wealth? I don't know many who have, and so the more I acquired, the less satisfied I became. I couldn't understand why this moment of peace and fulfillment was eluding me because I had bought into the American Dream, and I thought at some point, like a good stock, a dividend would be paid. But, whatever I did on one day wasn't good enough. I had to do more the next day. And, whatever I did the next day didn't satisfy. This is the American Dream isn't it? It gets perverted real quickly and we never seem to have enough.

Within three months of my thirtieth birthday, a radical event happened in my life, I was fired. Now, I don't recommend this for everybody. For me however, career and position and all of the "stuff" had become the center of my life. There was no room for anything else. Yes, I was married, and yes, I had children, but the real driving force in my life was to be successful, to be well known. Why? Not because I felt I was greedy or egotistical, but I really felt that achieving these things would bring peace, fulfillment, meaning, and purpose to my life. And yet, the more I got, the less peaceful I felt, and the more I had to have. People I know who have been on drugs say that my experience with success and fame is similar to theirs. You take drugs and you get high, but it is never enough. You come down and you have to have some more. My drug was fame, money, power, and success. By the way, if you are ever working for NBC and it's Friday afternoon and the boss says, "Have you got a minute?"

It's all over for you. Just thought I would tell you.

Funny thing about Washington, bad news travels quickly. People whom I thought were my friends didn't return my phone calls. People I thought really cared about me couldn't be found. I was virtually alone in the city of my birth, and it was a very sobering experience.

I couldn't find another job. I had to move back to Houston, Texas. I took a $20,000 a year cut in pay and sold the nice house and the big car. You know the person who said to be nice to people on the way up because you are going to meet them on the way down? Well, he knew what he was talking about. Instead of steak every other night, Chef Boy Ar Dee became a regular guest at our dinner table.

Well, eventually things worked out, but not before some other significant things happened in my life.

I'd always had a religious awareness, but I had never known anything beyond religiosity, the externals. I had done the religious things to please my parents. When I was twelve years old, I walked down an aisle, I signed a card, I went down dry and came up wet. I had my "fire insurance policy" in my back pocket so I wouldn't f-r-y when I died, and I spent some time in the most uncomfortable form of seating devised by man—other than the Indian nail bed—something called a P-E-W. (I don't know why they called it that.) I listened to a bunch of boring sermons full of do's and don'ts, mostly don'ts. You've heard them, I'm sure: don't drink, don't smoke, don't chew, and don't go with girls who do. Don't dance, don't play cards, don't go to movies, shut yourself away in some sort of convent and wait till you die. (Making sure your funeral costs are paid off, of course, ninety days same as cash!) Then, you'll go to the bright, pearly gates in the sky, and someone will issue you a harp, a white robe, some sandals, a halo, and a set of wings, and you'll walk down streets of gold singing, "A-m-a-z-i-n-g Grace!!"

I knew about God. I'd seen His picture. He was white, had a beard, and reached out across the Sistine Chapel ceiling to touch a guy with a lot of muscles who looked a lot like Burt Reynolds. But, He was w-a-y up there, and I was way down here and I couldn't relate. Oh, I'd gone to Sunday school a couple of times, usually taught by little old ladies with their hair in buns and orthopedic shoes. They pointed to places on maps that I didn't know existed and never expected to visit. It was all old and remote, and this was the closest I got to this Person, this idea called God.

I was now busy working six or seven days a week, going three or four weeks at a time without a day off. I was afraid to go on vacation for fear that somebody with a greater drive than I had might step in and beat my time and take my place on the ladder of success.

My wife was feeling this emptiness as well in her life, not only because she was on a similar search, but because I wasn't home much. She began doing a little volunteer work for something called "The National Prayer Breakfast" in Washington. She came home one day and was surprised to find me home in the middle of the day, but it was near tax time and

I was trying to remember the names of the kids for the deductions. She said she had met some people that she thought I would like to meet. Now, I didn't have time for anybody who couldn't boost my career, but she persisted. (Then I would have called her a nag, so you can see how far I've come!) They were located on my way to work, so I agreed to meet her friends to get her off my back. (I only said the first part to her, of course.)

I went down to this place and it wasn't a religious building. It was The American Security & Trust Building, a bank. They had a little private meeting room there just about a block from the White House. (In those days you could get within a block of the White House without all of the blockades.) I heard a Federal Judge stand up that morning, an amazing thing, and talk about the possibility of everybody in that room having a personal relationship with Jesus Christ. (In attendance that morning were a White House aide, a vice president of one of our major corporations, and some other elected officials.)

Now, I had gone to a building called church; you know, when I felt guilty about something I'd done on Saturday night or when there was a girl I wanted to impress. I'd thrown a few pennies in the plate, drank a little grape juice, sang some hymns—I could rarely hit the high notes—and then went home, but I had never heard of the phrase—a personal relationship with Jesus Christ. I didn't say much that morning. People who know me think that was unusual.

A week later the same man called me and invited me to a Bible study. I thought, "You guys have really gone nuts. Who can understand the Bible? It's full of thee's and thou's and whithersoever's and wherefore's and thou arts." The only person I knew who had talked like that was Shakespeare, and he had been dead for 400 years. But, these people were smart, and they invited me to a big house in McLean, Virginia with some very fashionable and successful people. How big was this house? Well, this house was so big they had a five-car garage. This house was so big they had a children's wing and only two kids. This house was so big it was a toll call from one end to the other. I mean we are talking a *big* house.

That night I met a United States Senator, the Chairman of one of our political parties, and some other successful men and women. They were articulate, successful, and good-looking people—people to whom I could relate. I thought, "Whoa! What are all these people doing here? They don't look religious."

You see, I thought God was for the crippled, the intellectually, emotionally, socially, and career crippled who couldn't really cut it in life. I figured they needed to lean on God as an excuse for getting up in the morning. I mean I had talent, I had looks, I had ability, I had a drive, and I was working on humility, but I figured four out of five wasn't bad. If I ever needed Him, I supposed I could find Him and He would help me. The rest of my life was for me to handle.

That evening I heard Dick Halverson, who was later to become my pastor and then the Chaplain of the United States Senate, read from a modern paraphrase called *The Living Bible.* I had an experience that night that was very similar to an experience I often had in high school when I had studied for a test and thought I had done very well. I would ask the "A" student, who was always a girl, "What did you put for number four?" and this cold, clammy feeling would come over me as I realized I had missed number four, and not only that, numbers one, two, and three as well.

As he read from the Bible, this same feeling came over me. I thought I was a big-time journalist. I was smart. If a politician made a claim, I'd look into it. If a business person asserted something to be true, I would investigate. But, like a lot of you, perhaps, I had never intellectually and honestly even opened this book called the Bible and read it for myself. Oh, I did once when I was ten years old and my grandfather had said he'd give me a silver dollar if I memorized the twenty-third Psalm, but that was the last time I ever seriously considered anything in this book that millions of people say contains so much wisdom.

After that evening I located one of these *Living Bibles* and said, "Okay, God, if you're really there, speak to me." I learned some remarkable things from reading that book on my own. I learned that everything I had been searching for in my career—the acceptance, the love, the reason for living, the value of my life—was something God was offering me. He loved me with a kind of love that I could never find in externals, the acquisition of money, things, power, fame, or position. All of these things I could have in a relationship with God who loved me with a kind of pure love that I could never find on this earth.

Then I found the second thing. I found out something about myself that was at least as profound. I learned that I was not perfect! My wife had been telling me this for years, but, you know, you kind of put it away and say, "Well, you just don't know me as well as I do." But, God told me I wasn't perfect, too. In fact, he told me I was a sinner. I really rebelled against that word because nobody is a sinner anymore; we're dysfunctional, right? You can kill your parents in L.A. like the Menendez brothers and throw yourself upon the sympathy of the jury because you're an orphan. Nobody does anything bad anymore because there's no such thing as bad or good. And, just for the sake of an argument, if we acknowledge that maybe there are some bad things, we're not personally guilty or accountable. If we do anything wrong, it's because we didn't get the dog we wanted when we were four years old, or we grew up on the wrong side of the tracks, we're the wrong race or the wrong gender. Nobody is personally guilty or accountable for anything.

As I examined myself, I realized that there was a flaw inside me. I had arguments with my wife, at times I was insensitive to my children, or I sometimes said a cross word to people who were simply doing their jobs. Why did I do this? It was because of this flaw that keeps me from being perfect.

The third thing I learned was that there was a tremendous gap between this holy, perfect God and myself. I learned that, no matter how many good things I did—serving on the hospital board, contributing money to worthy charities (these are all good, I'm not taking away from their value)—good deeds were not good enough to bridge this gap. I could not bridge this gap no matter how many good works I did. And yet, this kind of love that God demonstrated towards me was so wonderful, so unlike anything I could experience on this earth, that He provided a way for me to be close to Him. He took the initiative to do this although He was the offended party and although I had rebelled against Him.

In most courts of law—Los Angeles notwithstanding—if you're accused of a crime and you confess, the judge declares you guilty and imposes some kind of sentence, even if it's parole. But, in God's court, when you declare yourself guilty before God, He provides the means by which you may be pardoned. What a contrast!

This leads me to the fourth thing I learned. I learned that God loves me so much that He sent His Son to die for me. John refers to Him as the "Lamb of God who takes away the sin of the world," (John 1:29) not only universally but personally. Those with a Jewish background understand what the lamb represents. On the Day of Atonement, Yom Kippur, the Jewish people were to bring a spotless, unblemished lamb into the temple of the priest to sacrifice. This wasn't because the lamb was holy, it was a picture of the lamb that God would send. Remember the sacrifice that Abraham was provided so he would not have to slay his son, Isaac? These are pictures, these are images so that when the Lamb of God came we would not miss Him.

As I began to read, my eyes opened. I am constantly amazed every day at what God is doing. People often ask, "What are your goals five years from now?" I don't have any. I tried running my life, God's doing a much better job. I'll let Him do it, thank you very much.

I said a while ago that we are arrogant because we think we've figured out everything in life. Solomon, it is said, was the wisest man who ever lived. Solomon found that, apart from a relationship with God, all of the things the world had to offer were meaningless. He tried wisdom, he found that to be meaningless. He tried pleasure and he found that to be meaningless as well.

Solomon concludes this way in Ecclesiastes, "So I hated life." Do you know that the number one cause of death among teen-agers today is suicide? Teen-agers with everything to live for are killing themselves at a greater rate than ever. Why? "I hated life," Solomon said, "because the work that is done under the sun was grievous to me. All of it is meaningless, a chasing after the wind. I hated all the things I had toiled for under the sun because I must leave them to the one who comes after me."

A few years ago my wife and I were at a party at the British Embassy in Washington, a very fashionable place with beautiful grounds. It was a spring garden party. The ladies were beautifully dressed in print dresses and straw hats. There were military attachés from other nations, a Supreme Court Justice, and a U.S. Senator in attendance. It was a very nice party. When we left, we drove down Foxhall Road, one of the more fashionable streets in Washington with million dollar-plus homes. A sign caught my eye, a little sign in a yard. It looked like a "for sale" sign but as I got closer to it, it was not. It had only two words on it and an arrow. The words were "estate sale."

I thought to myself, "All of the *things* these people had toiled for—the furs, the jewels, the house, the oriental carpets, the goodies of life—were that day being sold by total strangers at auction and bought at a discount by people the now dead owners had never even met."

I thought once again of that incredible verse, that wonderful, truthful, and sobering verse, "What shall it profit a man if he gains the whole world but loses his own soul?" (Mark 8:36). This is the ultimate reckoning and accountability, ladies and gentlemen. I have never been to a seminary; I'm not even religious. I don't believe in religion. I think religion has been one of the most destructive forces in human history. God is not the author of religion, and Jesus Christ did not come to establish a religion. He came to reestablish a broken relationship with an infinite, personal, objectively existing God.

To this, I can relate. Jesus had nothing to do with all the other stuff—the majorities, the coalitions, the religiosity, the denominations. These are the creation of humanity. Some of it is good and some of it is not so good, but all of it is irrelevant. The Baptists aren't getting you to heaven, the Catholics aren't getting you to heaven, the Presbyterians aren't getting you to heaven, and the Lutherans aren't getting you to heaven. Whatever your name is or wherever it was on a cradle roll is not going to get you into heaven. That's not according to my authority; that's according to what I read in God's Word. I've done nine books, God only did one. He got it right the first time.

Most of us don't have the intellectual integrity to explore what He has done. I write about ideas. Sometimes I'm wrong. Readers of my column write me and tell me all the time. But, God is never wrong. How could He be? Why would He send wrong information that would cause us to get lost on the journey home?

A few years ago at the National Prayer Breakfast in Washington, a very unusual speaker said some very unusual things. I've never heard someone at this level talk so openly about the things that James Baker, the Secretary of State of the United States, talked about that day. And, I'll conclude with this.

The Secretary of State said, "Most importantly, having a position of power does not bring inner security or fulfillment. That comes only by developing a personal relationship with God, which for me is personified by Jesus Christ. Inner security and real fulfillment comes by faith, not by wielding power in a town where power is king."

He went on to say that those of us who believe know only too well that faith more often than not does not come easily. It takes work. "When I look back on my own journey of faith, I can see that real growth began when I started reading God's Word as a young man," he said. "Romans 10:17 in the New Testament says, 'Faith comes by hearing, and hearing by the Word of God.' The Scriptures also teach that God loves me and accepts me as I am. He loves me as I struggle and even as I fail to become the man He wants me to be. Once upon a time I felt I had to earn God's love, but now I know, because the Bible tells us, that it is faith and not works or accomplishments that makes us acceptable in God's sight."

He went on,

> In 1986, I met with a group of diplomats gathered in Washington for the National Prayer Breakfast. One of them asked me what I felt was the most important thing I had learned since being in Washington. I told him it was the discovery that temporal power is fleeting. I told him about an experience I had early one morning a few years earlier when I was White House Chief of Staff. As my driver turned our car into the northwest gate of the White House, I looked down Pennsylvania Avenue and noticed a man walking alone. He was someone many of you would have recognized, a Chief of Staff in a previous administration. There he was alone, no reporters, no security, no adoring public, no trappings of power, just one solitary

> man alone with his thoughts. That mental picture continually serves to remind me of the impermanence of power and position. That man had it all, but only for a time. That memory puts my own life in perspective. When I leave Washington, what will remain?

We might extend that and ask when we leave this life what will remain and, more importantly, where will we go and how do we know? The Scriptures say Jesus is "the way, the truth, and the life, and *no one* comes to the Father but through Him." (John 14:6) Unless we have a personal relationship with God through Jesus Christ, according to Scripture, we will not go to heaven. That's not on my authority, that's on His. He proved Who He said He was; He rose from the grave. Let one of the so-called other religious leaders try that.

I want to give you an opportunity to do something very profound. Again, I'm not ordained, I'm a journalist. Some people think that's at the other end of the perspective, but God was gracious enough to me that, even though I was yet a sinner, He sent Jesus to die for me personally.

You do have to deal with the fact that you are going to die, and you need to be certain where you are going. Meanwhile, you can have meaning and purpose for living, a reason for getting out of bed in the morning, and you can restore broken and lost relationships with the power that God will give you through His Son and through His Spirit. He'll do that for you if you'll let Him. He's done the heavy lifting. All you have to do is receive His gift.

All of you are familiar with journalists who prey (p-r-e-y), but we're going to have the other kind right now. So let's p-r-a-y:

If you agree with me and agree with God about yourself, I invite you in the silence and privacy of your own heart to repeat these words after me:

> Dear God, I confess to you right now that I am a sinner and deserve your judgment. I repent, I turn from and I am sorry for my sins,

and I ask your forgiveness. Now, God, I invite your Son, Jesus Christ, into my life. Thank you for forgiving me of my sins because of what He did for me. Thank you for loving me. And now God, please, help me to get some of my questions answered and thank you that You've answered the most important one.

In Jesus name,
Amen.

Chapter Four

Russell O'Quinn

I know when you hear the words "test pilot" you automatically think of someone like Tom Cruise. I'm terribly sorry to disappoint you, but if it will help your disappointment, I used to look a lot like Robert Redford. In fact, I opened a magazine recently and saw a picture of him without make-up, and it gave me perverse pleasure to see that he's beginning to look a lot like me!

I'm known as a 'dinosaur' in my industry. I'm past the age of sixty and still flying and testing advanced jet fighter aircraft full time, and it's a thrill! On occasion, I engage in air combat maneuvers with younger pilots who are graduates of schools known as "Top Gun" and "Red Flag." It's fun to go out there and "dogfight" with these youngsters half my age, and it does great things for my ego, when once in a while I overhear them tell a fellow pilot, "Don't go out there and fool with that old man unless you want to be embarrassed!"

Aviation has occupied a major share of my life. In fact, my fascination with it began at a very early age. You can believe this or not, but I knew what I wanted to do at the age of five.

My early years were spent in Southern California during the depression of the thirties. My parents were like a lot of folks back then who didn't have very much money.

When I was five, my Mother had an occasion to be away for a couple of weeks, and my Dad was left with a five-year-old toddler and a whole lot of things he needed to do. He did well until about the middle of this two-week period when he decided he needed to finish roofing the house. Now, being a creative individual, he took me up on the roof and nailed the seat of my pants to the roof. And, I'll tell you, a ten-penny nail is a very effective baby sitter. I'm sure he thought he had a captive audience and that I was going to learn something by watching him, but he was mistaken. This house was right under the final approach to the local airport, and I spent the entire afternoon watching the airplanes fly overhead. Thus began my love affair with the airplane.

I can still see those airplanes, so strongly were they impressed on my young mind. I built model airplanes. I read everything I could get my hands on, and every now and then I'd sneak away and go to the local airport, hang over the fence, and watch the real thing take off and land. When I became a teen-ager, I began to make noises about learning how to fly. That's when things came to a screeching halt.

I suddenly discovered that both of my parents were terrified of aviation. They had been putting little road blocks in my way all along, but I had not recognized it. And, so began some outright arguments over my love of aviation and my determination to learn to fly. Finally, we arrived at a compromise that I would be allowed to work after school at the local airport as a line boy, a sort of all-purpose grease monkey. So important was this compromise, that my Dad took me to work the first day and stopped at the entrance to the airport and pointed to a sign that said Flying Lessons, $12.00 an hour.

"Son," he said, "I want you to know that your Mother and I have agreed to this job with the specific understanding that you do not avail yourself of what's written on that sign."

I was fairly devious even at that early age, and so I said, "Yes, sir, I agree not to spend any money on flying lessons." True to my word, I didn't; I just took them in compensation for my work. Since there was no money changing hands, I thought I was at least staying within the boundaries of honesty.

In those days, you could learn to fly, solo, and get your license at an early age without a lot of regulations or your parents' consent. It took me about a year and a half, and my parents didn't know.

The only mistake I made was the day I got my private license. I decided to celebrate by "buzzing" the house. Somehow my Mother knew who that was. You've heard of teen-agers being grounded? I'm a living example of a teen-ager literally grounded for six months.

The family arguments began all over again with the strife and tension. I guess they finally realized that this aviation thing was not going to go away, and they agreed to allow me to continue my first love.

I knew I wanted aviation to be my life's work, but I didn't know how to get into professional aviation. There were a couple of things that happened about that time that sort of steered me, you might say, and one of them was a Hollywood movie. It was entitled *Test Pilot,* starring Clark Gable, Spencer Tracy, and Myrna Loy. Clark Gable and Spencer Tracy were busy testing the very latest airplanes of the day. It was a thrilling portrayal of a new area of aviation that peaked my interest. I'll bet I went to see that movie a hundred times. It drove a stake in the ground for me to focus my sights, but it still didn't tell me how to get there.

Another thing that occurred about that time was a little more practical; they started up the National Aerobatic Championships again. (They had been canceled during World War II.) They were held in Florida each year, and the best pilots in the country competed. Whoever won was really "Mr. Somebody" in aviation. I figured if I could get good enough and someday win, I would be on my way. So I began to study aerobatics.

About three months after I began, I was in the air at 3,000 feet practicing eight point slow rolls and other maneuvers, when my Dad happened to be driving along on the ground underneath the area. He looked up and somehow or another knew who was flying. I was grounded all over again.

Now, I wasn't terribly swift on my feet in those days, but I did notice that right after my flying became public, as it were, a change was occurring in our family routine. Every summer during school vacation, we were uprooted from California and taken to Oklahoma. My grandparents were pioneers in the Sooner state. They went in with the Land Rush of 1889 and homesteaded large sections of land right around Oklahoma City. In fact, my grandfather established the first commercial dairy in the state. It wasn't any tremendous empire, but it was a marvelous place for a city kid like me to ride horses, swim in the streams, sleep out under the stars, and spend time with aunts, uncles, and cousins. When I got over my upset of having to leave aviation for three months, I enjoyed those summers.

Early on, I identified a seemingly weird aunt. This woman did strange things, at least they were strange to me. She prayed out loud before she ate her meals at dinnertime, read her Bible right out in front of everybody, and went to church two or three times a week. Now, that made her strange to me because those things were missing in my growing-up period. My Mother and Father were fine, moral people, and we went to church maybe once a year, but I was always afraid this aunt was going to corner me and pour religion down my throat. So, I stayed as far away from her as I could . . . until my last trip.

I had just graduated from high school and my aunt succeeded in cornering me.

When she sat down beside me and began to talk I thought, "Oh boy, here it comes."

But, she had a quality known as wisdom, and she began in this way, "You know, if you're ever going to amount to anything in this aviation profession, you ought to go to college. You ought to get an aeronautical engineering degree."

I was going to stop her right there because I wanted to go to Florida and enter the aerobatic competition, but before I could get that out of my mouth, she "dangled a carrot" I couldn't resist.

"If you'll go, I'll pay for the first year's room, board, and tuition." She added.

So, I thought, "Well, what could I lose? I'll try it for a week or two, and if I don't like it I can always leave." I should have known better when she already had the college picked out, but nonetheless, that September I found myself standing on the campus of a small college in the Ozark Mountains of Arkansas.

After I registered and got settled into the men's dormitory, I decided to go out and explore the campus. The first thing I noticed was a bunch of "nuts" carrying Bibles under their arms, and I knew instantly that my aunt had betrayed me. I had fallen into a hotbed of religion. I turned around and marched back to my room determined to pack and leave the next day. But, a strange thing occurred that evening. Little by little, I ran into fourteen other guys of the same ilk as me. They, too, had been conned into coming to this nuthouse, and saw the same sights as I did. They, more or less, were coming to the same conclusions. You know how birds of a feather sort of flock together. Well, we had all found each other by about two o'clock in the morning.

Instead of leaving, we decided it might be more of a challenge to form a club and see what kind of devilment we could create for these nuts and the faculty of this institution. That's when my college education really began.

I learned things you wouldn't believe, most of them not on the school curriculum.

I was a fast learner, I identified my major field right off the bat. I majored in mistakes people made. I learned that the first person who had made a mistake was my aunt. She had put the entire year's worth of room, board, and tuition in my hands. She was a wise woman, but not too smart on that. Money does strange things to people, you know, and it sure did to me. It opened up whole new vistas of opportunity. In fact, I began a research program with my new-found wealth, several of them, in fact. In my research I discovered a major organization that was making some mistakes—the United States Government. I could buy a fairly advanced Army training aircraft, war surplus, for about half of the amount my aunt had given me. So, I made a snap decision and decided I'd pay for the first half of the year's room, board, and tuition. We'd let the second half worry about itself. And so, I bought an airplane.

Another discovery was an airport, owned by the college, and located just below the campus. They didn't know what to do with it, but I did. I flew the airplane to campus, and now I had the basis for a dual educational pursuit—the continuation of my study of aerobatics *and* the pursuit of a college education.

I should pause to tell you that my aerobatics studies did have some method to them. In those days, each pilot could select the series of maneuvers he wanted to perform in competition and then form them into a routine. The only limitations were that they all had to be performed within a very short period of time and also within a very concise air space. I worked hard on my maneuvers. These maneuvers are very difficult to learn. They're even more difficult to perfect to competition level. I didn't want to give up the inertia or the edge. I was running short of cash, however.

Many of you who are aviators can appreciate this. I'm one of the first, if not the first, to develop a system whereby an advanced aircraft engine can be modified to run on automotive fuel. Now, the thing that motivated me to do this was my shortage of cash of course. In further research I discovered that the State of Arkansas left a variety of vehicles, used for roadwork, unattended on weekends. I formed some of the guys into what's known as "the fuel brigade," and suddenly I had all the fuel I needed. You laugh, but fuel is very necessary if you're going to fly airplanes. I did pay the guys back for their fuel acquisition duties by letting them ride in the back seat with me when I practiced my maneuvers. We won't mention reimbursing the State.

Low altitude maneuvers were allowed in competition in those days, and I selected the two I was going to use. The first one was going to be my entry maneuver, the very first maneuver performed upon leaving the field where the competition was held. It was a low altitude, very violent maneuver that went like this: After doing the run-up at the end of the runway, I'd turn around and line up with the runway, take off climbing to about twenty feet, at this very low altitude retract the landing gear and the flaps, accelerate out to the maximum speed obtainable, pull up vertically, do a vertical snap-roll, pull out onto a precise heading, and sort of disappear off into the sunset. I did it every time I left the airport, and it became my signature. Groups of students and faculty would gather on the college hill to watch this amazing display. The students loved it although the faculty had other thoughts about it. Nonetheless, there wasn't any doubt as to who was leaving the airport.

During some recreational flying with the members of my "fuel brigade," I discovered that the Ozarks have rolling and forested hills. I found that one could fly through the ravines below treetop level for an extended period of time. Sooner or later, a dead end appeared and that made it kind of fun. In fact, I invented the airborne version of the game "chicken" doing this. We would fly through these ravines, come to a dead end, and whoever grabbed the stick first to pull above the treetops—an airplane has two sets of controls—was the chicken. I used to win almost every time, but I wound up putting a few green stains on the bottom of the airplane in the process.

It was during the game of chicken that I made another discovery. Did you know that a cow can outrun a horse? I made this discovery quite by accident one day. In coming out of a ravine, instead of a dead end, there was a large pasture populated with a variety of horses and cows. I want to tell you, a properly motivated cow will outrun a horse any day of the week. There's just something about a Pratt & Whitney R-1340 aircraft engine coming at a cow at 150 miles an hour that does strange things to their psyche.

By now, I was really beginning to enjoy college. I was staying just ahead of the campus cops—that's what we called the faculty—not doing anything too outrageous, and I was keeping my grades above redline. I survived, that is, until one day when things came to a screeching halt again!

I ran head-on into an individual who had all the characteristics of my aunt. This happened when somebody discovered I was not taking a required course. I thought I had gotten away with it, but they found me out. Guess what the course was—Bible, and I had to start taking the course.

The individual I'm referring to was the Bible professor. I would sit way in the back of his class, and the instant class was over I would escape out the back door. One day I was almost out the door and there he stood. How in the world he ever got from the front of the class to the back that quickly, I'll never know, but he collared me and I thought for sure he'd discovered some major infraction of which I was guilty. But instead, he invited me to his home for dinner and said he and his wife would like to get to know me! I wasn't fast enough on my feet to think up a good excuse, so I agreed.

They were a cordial couple and dinner was marvelous. Afterwards he invited me into his study to talk. Now, I was way ahead of him and knew what was coming, and I was prepared to turn him off. But, there were two things that prevented me from doing this. After we were settled in his study, I suddenly became aware, for the first time in my life, that I was confronted with someone outside of my immediate family who cared about me. The second thing that struck me, was that I admired this man. He was very knowledgeable, capable, and he had taken the time out of his busy schedule to spend time with me. No one had ever done that before, so I decided to listen, and I was surprised at what he said.

"You know," he began, "you're in an institution of higher learning, and sooner or later you are going to be confronted with a course that will teach about the origins of the universe, the origins of the earth, and the origins of mankind. Many years ago I gave a great deal of study to these subjects, and I'm going to give you the benefit of what I learned."

He paused and then proceeded, "After studying these subjects extensively, I came to the conclusion that there are only two possible basic premises. One premise holds that eons ago there was a cataclysmic explosion that began it all, and since that time the heavens and the earth, mankind, and all living things have been formed by a process known as evolution."

He continued, "The other position holds that there is an Almighty, all knowing, all capable God who created the Heavens and the earth, and mankind in particular."

"After much study in related sciences, I was awed by the creativity and genius of design I saw, and I came to the conclusion that there had to be somebody behind all of this. One of the things that drove me to that conclusion was a single word. It is the only word that adequately describes the theory of evolution and that word is accident. I could in no way reconcile what I saw in my study of the physical sciences with 'accident' so I came to believe that indeed there is a God."

He went on and described how God in the beginning had created man and because man disobeyed God, he became separated from God. But, God desired a reconciliation. Then he introduced me to Someone I had only known in a profane way, Jesus Christ. The minute he mentioned that name I became very uncomfortable. He described what Jesus Christ did 2,000 years ago and how He had accomplished that which was necessary for man to find his way back to God. His dying on the cross was necessary for man to have his sins forgiven and for man to have an eternal reconciliation with the God of Eternity.

Well, all of this was foreign to me and he knew it. Being a wise man, he then let me off the hook and walked me to the front door. Before I could escape out into the night, he added, "There's one more thing. I know you're uncomfortable and this may make you more so, but my wife and I care about you. We've been praying for you. Perhaps you have never had anyone pray for you."

As far as I knew, I hadn't.

He went on, "We're going to continue praying. We're praying that God will bring you to the point where you will recognize a very scientific fact, the fact that you're going to leave this life one day and you're going to stand before God and give an account of yourself. We're praying most of all that before that day arrives you'll come to know this Jesus Christ that I've been telling you about and receive the gift of eternal life that he has to offer."

I couldn't wait to leave, so I escaped back out into the night and went right back to staying one step ahead of the campus cops and continuing my dual education.

There were three other pilots in my ragtag group of friends. One of them began to bug me to let him fly my airplane. He'd never flown anything as advanced as this airplane, but since he was the head of my fuel brigade, I really couldn't think of any good reason to say no. So, I gave him several hours of training. He became proficient in the airplane and the day came to solo. We went out to the airport, did our walk-around inspection, and I helped him on with his parachute. We got up on the wing, and I watched him strap in and go through the start procedure. I tapped him on the shoulder, jumped down from the wing, and watched him taxi away. At the end of the runway, he did the run-up and the pre-flight checklist just like I'd trained him, turned around, and lined up with the runway, took off, and climbed to about thirty feet. He leveled off, retracted the landing gear and the flaps, accelerated out, pulled up, and tried to emulate the maneuver that he had seen me do so many times. At about 500 feet he lost control, pitched over, and dove straight into the ground at about 150 miles an hour.

I had never seen death before. To say that I was a shocked young man would be a gross understatement. I'll never forget that day as long as I live.

It hit me like a runaway express train: I was responsible. If anybody belonged in that pile of smoking wreckage it was me, not my friend; and I knew it. It never dawned on me that somebody might follow in my footsteps. I went back to my dormitory room and locked the door. Then I got down on my knees beside my bed and tried to pray. I'd never prayed before in my life. I didn't even know how to pray, so, I just cried," Oh, God, I can't handle what's happening here today!" Then a formal prayer came to my mind. I had learned it in the Bible professor's class, and I cried it out. "Oh, God, be merciful to me, a sinner, and save me for Jesus Christ's sake."

That night I discovered that, indeed, there is a God, for in those moments I felt a peace and calm that could only have come from Him, and I know he's a God of His promises because He answered my prayer that night. He performed a miracle. He literally changed my life, not just for a day or a month or a year, but he changed me forever.

Let me be quick to say that I don't claim to be perfect, not at all, but God literally performed a miracle that manifested itself in something that happened the very next day. I had a sudden desire to study the Bible. Now, if you had told me prior to that day that I'd *ever* have any desire to study the Bible, I'd have laughed in your face. But, as I began to read the Bible, I found a verse that described what had happened to me. Second Corinthians 5:17 says, "Any man who is in Christ becomes a new creation. Old things pass away and, behold, all things become new." And, that's exactly what God did for me that night.

Years later, I heard a southern preacher say, "When God saved me, he changed my *want to.*" And, that's exactly what God did for me; He changed my *want to.* My life hasn't been the same since.

I learned that I had misconceptions about being a Christian. I thought in order to become a Christian I had to become as good as my aunt, and I knew I could never "hack" that. I also thought I might need to attain the level of the

Bible professor, and I knew I would never reach those heights. In my study of the Bible I learned that no one can live a life commensurate with that which is necessary to be reconciled with the God of eternity. Only through that which Jesus Christ did for us on the cross 2,000 years ago are we able to be reconciled with God, the Father.

The other misconception was that I might have to become a preacher or a missionary and go off to some foreign land. I didn't know what those professions meant, and they worried me a great deal. But, God did not do that with me. He allowed me to continue in the profession that I loved so much. In fact, He's allowed me to go on and achieve every dream I'd ever had and then some.

Many years ago, I was selected as the project test pilot for an advanced weapon system. That weapon system was used recently in Desert Storm with great effectiveness. Most of you saw it on television, and I was privileged to be selected as the chief test pilot. When the time came to fly, I went out to the base at about 5:00 A.M. I suited up, briefed, and then strapped on the fire breather. I sat on the ground for two hours, functioning the system, telemetrying the data to a variety of receivers, and analyzing the data as it came back from them. When we were satisfied that the system operated properly, I started the engines and taxied to the end of the runway. As I climbed to 30,000 feet and leveled off, the sun came up. It was one of those beautiful days with azure skies and puffy white clouds. I had about ten minutes to get to the test area, so I had time to reflect. It hit me, as I sat there in awe of the marvelous and beautiful morning, that right that instant I was living every last dream I'd ever dreamed. Even Clark Gable never flew an airplane like this one.

Strangely, my education was increased again. Do you know what I learned? I learned that, when dreams come true, they're not all they're cracked up to be. Now, please, don't misunderstand me. Dreams are one of the joys of life and we are to pursue them, but unless God is the author of those dreams, there is a tragic disappointment awaiting you. Take it from one who has seen a lot of dreams come true. First, they will not satisfy the way you think, and they only lead to bigger dreams. Even further, they do not provide that deep, satisfying fulfillment that we thought they would.

When Clark Gable flew, he had the strings of a symphony orchestra playing in the background. I had sweat running out of my helmet and clear down to my boot tops. I wasn't looking forward to what I was going to have to do with this airplane in the next hour and a half, and suddenly, my dreams were not all they were cracked up to be.

Another thing I learned is that dreams become memories very quickly. Have you noticed? Some are over before we really enjoy them. And suddenly, we're looking back at them in disappointment.

Some dreams last longer, and I know that, but they are still transitory.

I have a friend who is a test pilot. He is well-known, and he's done much more than I have in this profession. He is retired now, and to me he is a sad man to be around. He and his wife are frightened of the future. Their lives are almost over and they know it. They sit talking about the good old days, reliving the golden years.

At this writing I am past the age of sixty. It is indeed a rarity to be flying the airplanes I fly at my age. They used to retire pilots mandatorily at an earlier age until they realized they were throwing away an awful lot of experience and knowledge. It is only because of what God has allowed me to accumulate in the way of experience and the gift of continued physical fitness that I'm still privileged to be flying a new concept jet fighter out on the *edges of the envelope.* I love it! I'm very much aware that the majority of my career is behind me, but I thank God that, when He met me in that dormitory room so many years ago, He gave me an eternal future. Retirement will not signal the end; it will signal a beginning.

The Bible says, "the eye has not seen nor ear heard, nor has it entered into the mind of man the things that God has prepared for them who love him." Forgive the vernacular, but we ain't seen nothing yet!

Have you noticed how fast our lives are passing? Oh, friend, the Bible says that the length of a person's life is but a mist. It appears for a little while in the morning and then it vanishes away. I laugh about this, but I hope you can identify with it. I've got this seemingly twenty-one year old brain running around in this sixty plus year old body, and it can't figure out how in the world the body got here so fast. My warning to you is deadly serious—if you've put all of your eggs in the basket of this world, you've made a tragic mistake. You really have.

Not long ago, I was asked to take the airplane I'm currently flying and spend two weeks giving flight demonstrations to eighteen young military pilots at a military airfield in the west. These pilots were selected from squadrons around the United States and were the "top guns" of their mission. As we gathered in the base auditorium on Monday morning, the commanding general for this mission gave the agenda and made the introductions for the two weeks. I was sitting out in the audience. Just four chairs down from me was a young major who had been selected as the temporary commander for these pilots.

He leaned over to one of my team and asked, "Who is the test pilot for the flight demonstrations during the next two weeks?"

My wise-guy associate answered, "It's the *old* guy sitting three chairs down."

I guess the major figured I couldn't hear, so he persisted, "Well, is he going to need help out to the airplane every morning? Did he bring a cane with him?"

I let this go in one ear, but not quite out the other.

When the general at the podium finished, it was our turn and we took up the remainder of the day giving critical briefings. As I concluded late that evening, I pointed to the twenty-eight year old major and said, "You're up first tomorrow."

After critical briefings the following morning, we got on board and strapped ourselves into our seats. I started the engines, closed the canopy, taxied to the end of the runway, and took off. We then climbed to the practice area. This new performance profile is about thirty minutes long. We do every maneuver seen in the movie *Top Gun* plus a whole lot more. Most of our maneuvers are vertical in both directions with entries of between five and seven positive G's with rapid reversals to two and three negative G's. We wound up doing 600 mile an hour, evasive tactics 100 feet off the desert floor, and concluded with a pop-up maneuver, went vertical, and pulled into an inverted position. We then selected a target, rolled in on it, and performed a simulated attack. After completion, I came off the target, did two victory rolls, and we were done. I can guarantee that if you haven't been doing this every morning after breakfast, it will uncage your eyeballs for you!

When I landed, the major was white as a sheet and had filled two air sick bags. It took two guys to help him out of the back cockpit. As we got to the bottom of the ramp, I couldn't resist, I leaned over and whispered, "You want to borrow my cane?"[1]

I admit that I was somewhat pleased with this preliminary debriefing of the major. It was a shock, however, to find that none of these young men was prepared for what was coming. It was a terrifying experience for each of them. It was terrifying because they thought they knew what was coming. You see, they were pilots. They knew how to fly. They knew the technology. They'd had the briefing materials for weeks. Some of them had even seen combat, but not one was prepared for what was coming. It taught us the necessity of being faithful to our briefings.

Now I'm writing this today to brief you, readers, every bit as if I were standing before you in full flying regalia and you were a young pilot about to embark on an important mission. But now, the subject is infinitely more important.

Like the pilots, there are some of you who think you know what's coming in your life, but you really don't. Please don't misunderstand me, I mean this in a loving way, not in an indicting way. You may have gone to church for years, sung the songs, prayed the prayers perhaps, or even read the Bible. You may have been wrapped in some sort of a marvelous, comfortable, spiritual cocoon, and you may have never considered that it was to *you* that the Bible says "All men have sinned and fall short of the glory of God," and "There's not a righteous man that walks on the face of the earth." You need to realize that it was to *you* that Jesus Christ said, "You must be born again." It was to *you* that the Bible says, "You must call upon the name of the Lord in order to be saved." Be aware that, we're the greatest people in the world for saying, "You know, Harry really needs to hear this." No, friend, I'm writing this to brief *you.*

There are some of you in an entirely different category. Somebody "conned" you into reading this book, and to you this is weird stuff and offensive. What I'm talking about may be "off the wall" and you don't want to hear about it.

I know exactly how you feel, friend. Shortly after I went to college, a girl invited me to a prayer meeting. I didn't really know what a prayer meeting was, but she was pretty and so I went. After a few minutes, the thirty students started praying around the circle, one after another. It didn't take a rocket scientist to figure out that they were eventually going to get around to me. I didn't have the foggiest idea what they were doing, and I wished I could have crawled under a table. Somehow or another, they managed to skip me. But, friend, if you're in this category, I can identify with you, I know exactly how you feel.

Would you give me just a couple more minutes? This is the most important subject you will ever consider in your life. I guarantee it.

Two thousand years ago a stupendous thing happened on this earth. The Creator of the universe took upon Himself the form of a man and walked amongst us. There are many who refuse to recognize Him, and that is a tragedy. They choose to call Him the Great Physician, the Great Teacher or the Great Philosopher. He was certainly all those things, but friend, He came for a much greater purpose. He came to purchase your redemption and mine. He came to reconcile us to the God of eternity, to accomplish that which we could not possibly accomplish ourselves. He came to pay a debt on your behalf and mine that we could never pay ourselves. You see, He was God in the flesh.

The Bible says, "There is no other name under heaven given among men whereby it's appointed unto man to be saved." Did you know that? I wish I had the eloquence to capture your attention at the level this subject warrants.

Here is a poor illustration. If I had you suited up today, you were standing with me beside an advanced experimental jet fighter, and I was briefing you on a particularly wild test flight you were about to take with me, I guarantee you would be hanging onto my every word. You would probably be terrified. That's understandable.

But, indeed, I am briefing you about another flight, one so important that it puts my illustration to shame. It's a flight you will take and it will be out of this world. I guarantee it will happen much sooner than you ever imagined. I don't care who you are, what your dreams are, or how much you are wrapped up in this world, this flight will come and you can't stop it.

I'm not suggesting a religion. This may surprise you, but this doesn't have anything to do with religion. It has to do with something infinitely more important. It has to do with your relationship to the God of eternity—or the lack of it. I am writing this to brief you about a Man, a Man like no other this world has ever known. This Man was God in the flesh. He absolutely shook the world. No one in the history of the world compares with Him. He willingly gave His life as a payment to purchase your salvation and mine. His name is Jesus Christ, and because it was not possible for death to hold Him, He arose from the dead. He sits at this very moment on the throne of eternity, and He offers you the free gift of salvation.

He declared, "I am the resurrection and the life, and he who believes in Me, though he were to die, yet shall he live."

I urge you, friend of mine, to accept Him as Savior and in so-doing receive His gift of eternal life.

You may be wondering, "What is this guy's angle?" There are many publications that pitch organizations, preach religion, or make appeals for money. I don't have any angles. In fact, I'm not even receiving authors' royalties for my portion of this book. I've put forth this effort for one purpose alone—for you to review your eternal destiny.

I close my briefing with the most important question you will ever ask yourself in this lifetime. I'd like you to remember that you heard this question from a test pilot, not a minister, preacher, or theologian. The question is based on the Scripture, "Whoever shall call upon the name of the Lord shall be saved."

Here is my question: Have *you* ever called on the name of the Lord and asked Him to save you?

If you are unable to answer this in the affirmative, and you feel God tugging on your heart, call on Him right now. Simply pray from your heart, wherever you might be, and if you mean it from the depths of your heart, I guarantee God will answer your prayer by changing your life and your eternal future.

If you got this far, thanks for reading my briefing to you!

To those of you who have received this gift and have embraced Jesus Christ as your personal Savior, let me divert for a moment and challenge you. Several years ago, I was in a jet fighter departing Edwards Air Force Base on my way to a civilian airport. My destination was socked in with a layer of clouds down to 500 feet. I had begun my instrument approach all the while taking the radar vectors. Then, the senior approach controller interrupted and asked me how much fuel I had left.

"Well, I've got plenty if I don't have to go fight a war," I replied.

"If you are willing, we'd like you to break off the approach. There's a light aircraft up above the clouds. He's low on fuel. He has no instrument rating, he has no experience in blind flying, and he's terrified. You're the closest source of aid we have. Would you go out and see if you can help him?" he asked.

So, I broke off the approach, and they vectored me until I was back on top of the clouds. I pulled up alongside this small airplane, a Piper of some type. I got his frequency and called him.

"Look to your left," I said.

When he turned his head, he saw this beautiful, modern jet fighter "sitting" out there right beside him. I had the landing gear down, full flaps, and everything but my hands out to slow down to his maximum speed. He burst into tears of relief.

I said, "I want you to calm down and do only one simple thing. I want you to follow me while you fix your eyes on my airplane. I'm going to make some gentle turns, and I'll tell you each time before I do. When I turn, you turn with me. We are going to descend into the clouds, but you will still be able to see me. I'm going to turn every light on, and you do the same. I'll keep watching to make sure I don't lose you."

We descended into the clouds, did some gentle maneuvers, lined up with the runway, and finally broke below the clouds. Suddenly, out of the mist appeared the flashing line of strobe lead-in lights and those brilliant twin rows of runway lights turned up to maximum brilliance. He was on his own again and landed safely.

After we landed, the man greeted me and embraced me with great emotion. Then, it struck me like a lightning bolt that God had given me a tremendous parallel.

I had just pulled up alongside someone who was lost and in danger of losing his life. And, here I was, in possession of a wondrous and powerful jet fighter, equipped with a dazzling array of the latest instrumentation and electronic navigation systems. What I had in my hands made child's play of the bad weather. In short, I had the answer to life in my hands!

The parallel is overwhelming! Friend, if you know the Lord Jesus Christ, you hold the answer not just to life, but to eternal life. I urge you to pull up alongside others who are lost and lead them safely home.

Notes

1. In fairness to the pilots, and for the benefit of readers who are familiar with military aviation, I will try to clarify an obvious paradox. These young men had never flown in a high performance jet fighter before, and it placed them at a decided disadvantage. Their mission is classified information, and all I can state is that it does not fall within the purview of frontline USAF fighter operators. The mission was studied after Vietnam, and it was very evident that the aircraft they had been flying was woefully inadequate. This program was to introduce them to both an expanded mission performance profile and high performance, agile aircraft to replace their current fleet. If you are a fighter jock reader, you would have rubbed your hands together in gleeful anticipation of introducing the uninitiated to the wonderful world of "ACM," just as I did. And yes, it was unfair, but it was a legitimate assignment, and somebody had to do it!

Chapter Five

Adolph Coors IV

In these next few pages, I'm going to share with you my family, our successes, our failures, our joys, and, yes, even our pain. The Adolph Coors name is one that I'm sure most people have heard. Some, rightly or wrongly, have said that our family is the embodiment of the American dream, a family which appeared to have it all together. Yes, it's a family probably much like yours with grand hopes and aspiring dreams. The Adolph Coors Company of Golden, Colorado, has grown into one of the largest breweries in the world today. The fact that the company was started in an old, abandoned tannery building in 1873 by my great grandfather and his business partner makes this one of the truly great success stories in America.

You can well imagine what this meant to our family in terms of prestige and material comfort. In September 1945, I was born into this not only successful, but very loving, caring, and close-knit family. One day in early 1960, however, that family fabric was violently ripped apart. My Mom, my two older sisters, my younger brother, the Coors name, and all that was the Coors legacy could not protect us. The Bible says, "He who provides for his life but takes no care for eternity is wise for a moment but a fool forever." In the Gospel of Matthew 16:21, we read: "What profit is there if you gain the whole world, but in the process you lose your soul? Or what can man give in exchange for his soul?"

The first fourteen years of my life were like a Norman Rockwell painting of a loving, close-knit family. As a young boy, I worshipped my Dad. In a real sense he was my god. I wanted to grow up to be just like him in every way. He was chairman of the board of our brewing empire, a semi-professional baseball player in his younger days, a gifted musician, a private pilot, an architect, an engineer, a pioneer in the development of skiing in Colorado, and a cattle rancher. But, all of these great accomplishments are not what stands out about my Dad. What I remember about this remarkable man is that he always had time for us, his family. He loved us and didn't mind showing us, and when necessary, he was stern and strong on discipline. What an unbeatable combination!

I had all the things money could bring and I had much, much more; two—loving parents, a beautiful home, and an above-average relationship with a younger brother and two older sisters. However, there was one missing ingredient to this beautiful Rockwell painting. Most every Sunday morning Dad or Mom would drive us kids to Sunday school and church, but I regret to say that I can't remember either of my parents going to church with us.

It was as if we were meant to find God, if He existed, on our own. I was like the little boy who was coming out of church one Sunday morning and was asked by his pastor how he enjoyed the service. The young lad replied, "Well, Pastor, the music was great, but the commercial was too long." A very wise man once said, "God often visits us, but we're seldom at home."

In 1958 my Dad grew tired of living in the city and decided to move our family from our home in Denver to our ranch in the foothills just west of the city. To me, it was the American dream home. But, life brings many changes. Some of these changes are sudden, some are gradual. Some are welcome while others bring tremendous grief. We mistakenly put our faith and trust in our immediate families, our relatives, our friends, and yes, even ourselves. However, God tells us, "All of my good gifts are to be received thankfully. But don't, don't put your faith and trust in them alone. Make me your rock bottom security." To make God our rock bottom security, we need to turn to the Old Testament and read Proverbs 15:26, "He who reverences the Lord has a secure fortress, and for his children it will be a refuge." And yet, life does not shout. It just runs out sooner than we think.

The date was 9 February 1960. I didn't see my Father that morning. It was his custom to awaken at 5:30, have an early breakfast, and then drive the twelve miles from our ranch to the brewery in Golden. It was a typically cold Colorado February morning. As my Father proceeded down the same road he traveled countless times before, he noticed a yellow 1958 Mercury parked alongside of the bridge just outside of Morrison. I imagine curiosity got the best of my Dad for he stopped his automobile and began to walk toward this vehicle to see if he could be of any assistance. What my Dad did not know, however, was that the occupant of the other car, an escapee from a prison in California, had been planning this morning for two years. As Dad approached, Joseph Corbett jumped out of his car and a violent struggle commenced. My Father, a strong, strapping German, apparently overpowered his assailant and fled, but as he ran to his car, he was shot repeatedly. Dad's body was stuffed into the trunk of the escapee's 1958 yellow Mercury, and it sped south. The time was 7:30 a.m. The only clues as to what might have happened were found by a passing milkman just minutes later. Those clues were my Father's ball cap, his eyeglasses found on the bank of the creek below the bridge, his car, and a spot of blood on one of the bridge railings.

Anger is only one letter short of danger. Some of you may remember reading about this horrible crime. It made national headlines for many months. It was one of those terrible tragedies people are interested in reading about as long as it happens to somebody else. We just don't believe it can ever happen to us.

Ironically, on 16 September 1933, a foiled kidnapping plot against my Grandfather, Adolph Coors, Jr., took place—the motive, $50,000. It was a foreshadow of things to come, the unfortunate prologue of the kidnapping of his son, my Father, some twenty-seven years later. In a real sense, the siege of this tragedy was laid in the earth three generations before when my Great Grandfather, Adolph Herman Joseph Coors, left his native Germany where he had worked and saved for several years to come to the United States. He immediately became imbued with the fine American tradition, "Never give up until success is attained." That thought never left my Great Grandfather, and it was his yardstick throughout his life.

My Great Grandfather was a workaholic. He devoted his entire life to his brewery. He nursed it along, even helping it to survive some serious flooding. His foresight was such that when prohibition came to Colorado in 1914, he had already established a pottery company and bottling works for some four years before it became a national law, he had been preparing for this eventuality. In fact, some experts today say that America would not have modern porcelain manufacturing had it not been for the foresight and ambition of Adolph Coors, Sr. In addition to this, he began to manufacture malted milk, and soon Coors became the third largest producer of this product in the United States. (He sold his malted milk to the Mars Candy Bar Company of Chicago.) Adolph Coors loved his business so much that, in the late 1800's, he built his home beside the brewery, and every male family member for the next two generations was born in that same home.

But, we need to remember what King Solomon tells us when he says that wealth is not the ultimate source of gratification. Neither did King Solomon find success and fame to be satisfying for him. Adolph Herman Joseph Coors was very prominent, highly respected, and loved in Golden and in the Denver area as well. After all, he was a success, but life does not shout, it just runs out sooner than we think.

On the morning of 5 June 1929, tragedy struck the Coors family. Adolph Coors, Sr., fell from a sixth story window of a downtown hotel in Virginia Beach, Virginia. The official story was that he had become very despondent over problems at the brewery, and after staying up all night with friends, Coors fell to his death.

In a similar light, O. J. Simpson once stated at the height of his career, "I stand in my house in Buffalo and sometimes get so lonely it's unbelievable. Life has been good to me. I have a great wife, good kids, lots of money, good health, but I'm so lonely and bored." I often used to wonder why so many rich people commit suicide. Money surely isn't a cure-all.

I don't believe that the burden was money as much as it was a drive for success with my Great Grandfather. Both my Great Grandfather and my Grandfather were perfectionists. However, the voids in their lives were never, nor could they ever, be filled by the family business. God never destines our lives to be fulfilled apart from a relationship with Himself through Jesus Christ, our Lord.

When the news of my Father's kidnapping reached my Grandfather, he handled it as he would any problem—systematically and without any outward expression of emotion. He simply called a board meeting to announce the news that my Father had been shot at 7:30 that morning on his way to work. I don't doubt that feelings of loss were deeply felt by my Grandfather; they were just kept inside. At the board meeting that morning and at every board meeting thereafter, my Grandfather left the chair next to his vacant. That simple gesture was his way of expressing his deep loss and respect for my Father.

My Great Grandfather and Grandfather should not be looked upon as bad people. They were fine men, highly esteemed and loved by all who knew them. Unfortunately, however, they were men who put their efforts and priorities in the wrong order, contrary to God's principles. I want to make the point again that my Dad, however, took time to be with us. When I come to the end of my life and my two boys think back to their childhoods, I wonder what they will remember? Will it be those kind of warm, loving days, those experiences of love between a father and a child; or will they remember a father who was never around—always running to another business meeting, playing another round of golf, or maybe flying on a jet plane to some far off place? I want them to remember me as a dad who took time to show his love and affection for them and for their mother.

Six weeks before Elvis Presley died, Elvis was asked by a friend, "Elvis, when you started playing music, you said that you wanted three things in your life. You wanted to be rich; you wanted to be famous; and you wanted to be happy. Elvis, are you happy"?

Elvis replied, "No, I'm lonely as hell. Rich and famous, but lonely."

At first, Elvis Presley's comments seemed almost offensive to me, but then the more I thought about it, I came to the conclusion that his comment was very well put. Hell, after all, is a very lonely place.

C. S. Lewis, one of this century's most gifted Christian writers, tells each of us, "If you live for the next world you get this one in the deal. But if you live only for this world, you lose them both."

Perhaps some of you are terribly lonely. For some very lonely people, hell begins right here on earth, one day at a time. Let's look at one day in a little different perspective. In one short day—only twenty-four hours—your heart beats more than 103,000 times. Your blood travels 168,000,000 miles. You breathe more than 23,000 times. You inhale 483 cubic feet of air. You eat more than three pounds of food. You drink approximately three quarts of liquid. You speak approximately 4,800 words. In this short span of time, however, how much time are we willing to devote to getting to know our magnificent God, the One who created us, by communicating with Him through prayer and reading his love letter to us, the Bible. For nearly thirty years of my life, I felt this same loneliness that Elvis Presley experienced, but I discovered that my loneliness was not a psychological problem. It was a spiritual problem simply caused by my separation from God.

Blaise Pascal, the famous French physicist, philosopher, and devoted Christian put it this way, "There's a God-shaped vacuum in the heart of every man which cannot be filled by any created thing, but only by God, the Creator, made known through Jesus Christ." We all do, indeed, have the God-shaped vacuum in our hearts. Something is missing. We are separated from God. Many try to fill this vacuum by working harder, making more money, or gaining more prestige and power. Yet, none of these things can fill that vacuum. Only a personal relationship with Jesus Christ can fill this void in our hearts. My many futile attempts at covering up this emptiness were useless because the emptiness always came back, only moreso. You see, rejecting God causes isolation and loneliness forever.

In a cemetery in England stands a grave marker with this inscription, "She died for want of things." Right next to it stands another which reads, "He died trying to give them to her."

Is any rich man truly content? Henry Thoreau once wisely said, "A man is rich in proportion to the number of things he can afford to let alone." Henry Ford, then chairman of the largest automobile company in the world said the following, "Work is my only pleasure. It is my work which keeps me alive and makes my life worth living at all. I was *happiest* when I was doing a mechanic's job."

Where is happiness found then? John D. Rockefeller, Sr., this country's first billionaire, said, "I have made millions but they haven't brought me happiness. I would barter them all for the days when I sat on an office stool in Cleveland and counted myself truly rich on three dollars a week." Lying near death, and given less than two years to live, at fifty-three years of age, John D. Rockefeller Sr., surrendered all he was and everything that he had to the Lord, Jesus Christ. He then lived to the age of ninety, but more importantly, to the glory of God. After his death, one of Rockefeller's accountants was asked to reveal how much money this great man left at his passing. The accountant said, "Mr. Rockefeller left all of it."

King Solomon warns about the dangers of materialism. Solomon was the third and last king of united Israel. He reigned forty years from 971 to 931 B.C. Solomon built Israel to its greatest geographical extension and material prosperity. He tells us to enjoy prosperity, but he also warns us not to wear the cloak of materialism too tightly. He tells us to wear it loosely. He is telling us that those who clutch can quickly crash. Those who grab will ultimately lose. Those who hold onto it will ultimately release it. This is not an attack on those who have money. This is an attack on the *lovers* of money, the greedy, and the materialists. Without God being at the very center of our lives, we cannot truly know fulfillment, contentment, and enjoyment. The poorest man is one whose only wealth is his money. No person can ever buy security. As Solomon put it so timelessly more than 2,900 years ago in the book of Ecclesiastes 5:10, "Whoever loves money never has money enough." Whoever loves wealth is never satisfied with his income. The materialist will never know the day when he or she can say, "That's enough." Materialism also gives a person a false sense of security. We need to understand that our actions, our philosophies of life, and, yes, even our material comfort can stamp an impression on our children that can cause ramifications within our families for generations to come.

J. W. Whitehead once said, "Children are the living messages that we send to a time we will not see."

Dads, we need to come to grips with the painful fact that much of our activity is nothing more than a cheap anesthetic to deaden the pain of an empty life. An unknown author wrote a poem directed to fathers that goes like this:

> Walk a little plainer, Daddy,
> Said a little boy so frail.
> I'm following in your footsteps,
> And I don't want to fail.
> Sometimes your steps are very plain,
> Sometimes they are hard to see.
> So walk a little plainer, Daddy,
> For you are leading me.
>
> I know that once you walked this way
> Many years ago,

And what you did along the way,
I'd really like to know.
For sometimes when I'm tempted,
I don't know what to do.
So walk a little plainer, Daddy,
For I must follow you.

Someday when I'm grown up,
You are like I want to be.
Then I will have a little boy
Who'll want to follow me.
And I would want to lead him
And help him to be true.
So, please, Daddy, walk a little plainer,
For I must follow you.

For each of us, life is passing by so quickly and will soon be gone. My challenge to you who are reading this today is to think about what is really important to you. How are you spending your life? What is worthy of your time? What are you doing that outweighs loving relationships with your spouse, your kids, and above all, your heavenly Father? John Henry Newman once said, "Fear not that your life shall come to an end, but rather that it shall never have a beginning."

Dennis Rainey, the founder and director of the Family Ministry of Campus Crusade for Christ recently stated, "Gentlemen, we need to ask ourselves this question, 'What do I want to win so badly that I am unequivocally unwilling to lose?' He goes on to say, "It had better be in our homes." Someday, when you die, they will put only one thing in that box—you. There are no U-Haul trailers attached to the hearse going to the graveyard. We can't take any of it with us. The only things that remain at our passing are the positive and negative influences, the right and wrong things we have done with our lives.

After my father was kidnapped, I prayed nightly in the loneliness of my bedroom to a God I didn't know in the personal way I know Him today, "God, please bring my Dad back to me." And, I would cry myself to sleep night after night. In September of that year, in a garbage dump twenty miles south of Denver, the remains of my Dad were discovered. The prayers I prayed those seven long months were not answered in the way I wanted. Nevertheless, I have learned, looking back over these many long years since that tragic day in 1960, that God, in His perfect wisdom, knows what is best.

At that moment in my life, I began the long process of understanding the importance of trusting God. Over these many, many years, I have come to learn that, when God does not immediately respond to the cries of His children, it is not because He doesn't hear the cries or feel our deep pain. Rather, it is because He wants to accomplish something far deeper in our lives.

As a young child I was blessed with a Mom who took time to share in my fun, to share in my secrets, and to play my games. Many a night she would stay a minute more to hear my prayers followed by plenty of goodnight kisses. Yes, without a doubt, I had a Mom who did those little things I asked of her, and, yes, much, much more. When our family got the news that Dad wasn't coming back to us, I saw a radiantly beautiful lady, my Mom, change before my very eyes. Hatred for the man who brutally murdered her husband began to consume her. Hatred for Joseph Corbett began to take over all of our lives. To make matters worse, I saw my Mom turn to the only crutch she knew; that crutch was alcohol. She soon began to drink excessively, and we, her children, were powerless to stop her.

There's something about grief that builds walls against communication between people, even family members. We just don't know what to say to someone who is hurting so deeply. There was growing inside of me a terrible emptiness. And, as the Coors men before me, I tried to fill that void in a number of ways apart from God.

I attended Mercer University in Macon, Georgia, but I was totally unable emotionally to handle the responsibility of being on my own. I majored in fraternity and sorority, and I minored in academics. I lasted but one year and did not return the following September.

I spent the next six years in the United States Marine Corps. With the name "Adolph Coors" and sporting a Marine burr haircut, I quickly discovered that I was going to have to become pretty tough very quickly in order to survive my tour of duty. I also came to realize that muscles, brawn, and pride were my only friends. I was literally consumed with task of proving to all around me that I was just as rough a Marine as they were. I was not going to fail this assignment. You see, there were too many people who were betting I wouldn't make it.

I began to mask my terrible insecurity by hiding behind a macho Marine image. I got involved in Karate and body-building. In the next seven years my weight went from 195 to 272 pounds. Yes, I was a man with twenty inch arms and a fifty-four inch chest, but behind those muscles was a tragically insecure person, screaming out for somebody to notice and accept him.

A few months before completing my tour of duty as a Marine, I learned from my Mother that my oldest sister, who was living in the Chicago area and the proud mother of a brand new baby boy, had just been diagnosed with incurable cancer. Within a little more than a year, Brook, my beautiful twenty-seven year old sister, died. Life does not shout, it just runs out sooner than we think.

When I was released from my tour of duty, I returned to Denver. In August 1967, I married my high school sweetheart, B. J. People are very funny. We spend money we don't have to buy things we really don't need in order to impress people we really can't stand. That accurately describes the first eight years of our marriage. Both B. J. and I mistakenly thought we could make it a happy and successful marriage by filling it with things. God, however, tells each of us that true happiness isn't for sale. Happiness doesn't come from owning things, but it is gained through a personal relationship with his Son, Jesus Christ.

Dr. Harold Sala in his marvelous book entitled, *And They Shall Be One Flesh,* writes the following; "I sometimes tell women that there are three words which are often in the mind of a bride. The *aisle* down which she will walk, the *altar* at which she will kneel, and the *hymn* which will be sung."

Putting these three words together, you have "aisle altar hymn," (pun intended) which is often what the bride has in mind when she marries her husband. And, B. J. was no exception to the above words. While she was trying to change me into a new person, I began to buy myself into materialism, hoping that things could fill my void. More importantly, I hoped that these things would impress our friends.

I thought owning a mountain home would be the answer for us. I promptly purchased a beautiful, lake front home in the mountains west of Denver. Every weekend, always surrounded by friends, we would spend two frantic days trying to find some meaning to this life. B. J. and I didn't feel comfortable alone with each other, so we always invited another couple to come along with us. As long as we were with other people, we didn't have to come to grips with our incompatibility.

We need to understand that there are many things money can't buy. Money can buy medicine, but not health. Money can buy a house, but not a home. Money can buy companionship, but not a friend. Money can buy entertainment, but not happiness. Money can buy food, but not an appetite. Money can buy a bed, but not sleep. And, money can buy a marriage license, but not a good relationship. Yes, money can even buy us a crucifix, but not a Savior, and money can buy us "the good life," but not eternal life.

I continued to carry the burden of the Coors name in the only way I knew, by striving first for success and then for money. I had the goal of becoming a millionaire by the time I was thirty years old. Huge losses, however, in both Colorado real estate and the commodities markets in Chicago quickly thwarted that goal. I was now staring personal bankruptcy right square in the face.

In August 1971, my wife and I were blessed with our first child, Adolph Coors, V. In 1972, I went to work for the Adolph Coors Company with the ambitious goal of becoming its youngest president, following in the footsteps of my Dad, my Grandfather and my Great Grandfather. In October 1973, I suffered a near-fatal automobile accident while returning home from the brewery one October morning. During the next two years, while in recovery from the accident, I began to take a hard look at my life. I was facing financial ruin and embarrassment and living in a marriage that was rapidly heading for divorce.

Who am I? Why am I? Where am I going? Why is it that so few of us ever try to find the answers to these three very important questions?

When my life was in total shambles and I despaired over ever amounting to anything, Lowell Sund, a vice president at Coors, and his wife, Vera, shared the claims of Jesus Christ with my wife and me one evening in our home. They opened up their lives to us, and they shared many verses of Scripture with us. Two that I remember very distinctly were Isaiah 53:6 and John 3:16. I'll paraphrase them in my own words. "We all, like sheep, have gone astray. Each one of us has turned to his own way and God has laid on Christ, the sin of us all." The other one which stands out in my mind very vividly is, "God so loved the world that He gave His one and only Son, that whoever believes in Him shall not perish but have eternal life."

Vera and Lowell Sund went on to explain to us that we were hopeless without God in our lives. We were hoping in the wrong things. We were casting about for something to pin our hopes on, and when that particular thing seemed to fulfill, we soon felt empty again. Hope in our lives was nothing more than wishful thinking. I learned also that our problem was that of hoping in things which give sensation. In other words, those things which we can experience with our five physical senses. The Bible, however, is very explicit about the dangers of putting one's trust in the tangible things of this life.

It was a week or so later that B. J. invited Jesus Christ into her life. I saw a significant change come over her. I knew deep down that she had something I desperately needed, however, I was convinced that the only answer left for me was divorce.

I moved out, leaving my wife of seven years and my four year old son behind. During those painful weeks of separation, God's Spirit began to work on me. For months I had tried to shut my mind off to what He was teaching me. My haven of freedom was a lonely room at the Denver Athletic Club. I thought for sure that a man who was finally set free from a marriage he didn't want, would certainly find happiness in the glamour of the single life. My glamour, however, consisted of a lonely dinner in the club dining room, followed by a lonely trip back to my room. This went on night after night, week after week.

While in my room each night I read a book Lowell Sund had given to me, a book with a marvelous little title, *Do Yourself a Favor and Love Your Wife* by Page Williams. In the pages of that great little book, I learned the importance of applying God's priorities, not mine, to my life. The most important priority is a personal, ongoing relationship with my heavenly Father through His Son, Jesus Christ. The second priority is a loving and meaningful relationship with B. J., my beautiful wife. Third, I needed to develop a closer relationship with my son, Shane. And finally, I needed to cultivate true friends. I hated to admit it, but I had none of the above. I was too caught up in what the world defined as success, and in the process, I was destroying those who were closest to me.

How was our separation affecting B. J.? She was lonely, but God was telling her that this was not the end of our marriage. While Lowell Sund was working with me, his wife, Vera, was working with her. My wife began reading a book called, *The Philosophy of Christian Womanhood.* That book helped her to make some important decisions about our relationship. For one thing, she physically tore up a long list of irritations about me. Boy, I guess that must have been quite a list. More importantly, she made a decision to quit trying to change me into the kind of man she could love and respect. She turned that responsibility over to God. After all, only God can truly change a person.

Finally, after a month and a half of separation, I called B. J. and asked if I could come home. I told her I truly wanted to become the husband she deserved and the father I had never been to my son.

I returned home committed to making my marriage all that God wanted it to be.

In the spring of 1975, I went to hear an evangelist speak at a large auditorium in downtown Denver. As I sat there, this man's words penetrated my heart with the claims of Jesus Christ. With tears rolling down my cheeks, I heard that salvation is found in no one else. "For there is no other name under heaven given to men by which we must be saved" (Acts 4:12). Jesus also told me that afternoon, "Behold, I stand at the door and knock. If you will hear my voice and open the door of your heart, I will come in and fellowship with you and you with me" (Rev. 3:20). That afternoon, by an act of my will, I opened my heart and life to Jesus Christ, and instantly Christ came into my life, filling the void that no person or possession had ever been capable of doing.

The truth of God's unconditional love for me began to flood my being. It penetrated my very soul. All I could do was sit, crying uncontrollably. I had never felt that kind of love. Suddenly, the one thing I had been looking for all these years was mine. My void was now totally filled, and for the very first time, my life had purpose and eternal destiny. As if by a miracle, those things that were once so important to me, no longer were. For the first time, my marriage to B. J. and my son took their proper place in my life. My highest priority, however, will always be my relationship with Jesus Christ. It became obvious to me that afternoon that a man is no fool who gives up that which he can never keep in order to gain that which he can never lose.

In July 1975, just prior to my Mother's departure for a short vacation to Aspen, Colorado, my wife and I both, on separate occasions, had the wonderful opportunity of sharing with her our newfound faith in Jesus Christ. Mom listened intently as we both told her how she could invite Christ into her life and allow Him to become her Lord and Savior. After a brief but meaningful conversation with both of us, she departed for Aspen, promising to call us upon her return in four days. Just three days later, however, Mom suffered a major stroke in the home of friends, and in a few short hours, Mom was dead. Remember, life does not shout, it just runs out sooner than we think.

We have the assurance that Mom did invite Christ into her life just prior to her tragic death. To those who know Jesus Christ, death is not a period, but a comma in the story of life. Let me be so bold as to say that the only person who has need of being scared of death is the one who is not ready for it. You are not really ready to live until you are ready to die. If you are not ready to die, you really ought to be scared.

One by one, God is removing those elements that are contrary to His will from my life. Over the prior seventeen years, I cultivated an intense hatred for Joseph Corbett, the man who brutally murdered my Father in 1960. Even after I gave my life to Jesus Christ, I could not rid myself of this hatred. Hatred, you see, is like a treacherous acid which cannot be poured without spilling it on the raw heart that holds it. Jesus Christ's own word tells us that if you forgive men when they sin against you, your heavenly Father will also forgive you. But, if you don't forgive others, your Father in heaven will not forgive your sins (Matt. 6:14-15). The New Testament also urges, "Do not take revenge but leave room for God's wrath. 'It is mine to revenge. I will repay,' says the Lord" (Rom. 12:19).

I can say from long experience that hate hurts the heart far more than the person being hated. In October 1977, a friend who was a committed Christian and was involved in a ministry to the inmates at the Calder State Penitentiary asked me to go with him into the prison for the sole purpose of forgiving Joseph Corbett for what he had done to my family. (In 1961, Joseph Corbett had been found in Canada and was sentenced to a life in prison at the Calder State Penitentiary for the murder of my Dad.) At first, I refused this man's request, but he kept asking, and I kept making excuses as to why I could not go with him. During this time, however, Jesus Christ was impressing upon my spirit the importance of forgiveness in my life. Even though I had given my life to Christ two years prior to this, I had been unwilling to surrender my hatred for Joseph Corbett to the Lord.

If anyone has a right to hate, it's Jesus Christ. While suffering the horrible agonies of crucifixion, the most hideous form of execution ever devised by man, Christ looked down at the very soldiers who had nailed him to the cross. In Luke 23:34 we read that He said, "Father, forgive them, for they do not know what they are doing."

In the weeks that followed, Jesus Christ began to reveal to me that, in spite of all my sin, He still went to the cross for me. In Romans 5:8 it says, "But God demonstrates his own love for us and that while we were still sinners, Christ died for us." As I began to comprehend this beautiful truth, it became painfully obvious that I had no right to hate another human being, not even the man who murdered my Dad. The desire to forgive involved a decision on my part, but I also knew that I was not capable of this kind of forgiveness. My answer to this dilemma was found as I read Philippians 14:13, where I found that I can do all things through Jesus Christ who gives me strength.

Three times in the power and strength of Jesus Christ. I traveled with my friend to the Colorado State Penitentiary at Calder to visit with Corbett, but each time Corbett refused to see me. After learning that he would not let me visit with him on my first visit, I wrote him a very short letter in which I asked for his forgiveness for the hatred I had been carrying for him for the past seventeen long years. In addition, I told Corbett that I had completely forgiven him for what he had done to me and my family. I concluded my short letter to him by saying that I would like to visit with him at some point in the future. I then asked the warden of the prison to deliver my letter to Joseph Corbett.

As I left that morning following my first aborted visit, I knew God had performed a wonderful miracle in my life. I was a free man, suddenly free from the hatred which had permeated my being like a cancer since my Father's brutal murder in 1960. In its place, I felt God's love and forgiveness, and they remain to this day. Even though I have not had the opportunity to visit personally with Corbett, my heart has totally reversed. Truly man's extremities are God's wonderful opportunities. Joseph Corbett has since been released from the Colorado State Penitentiary, and as of this time, I've had no contact with him. Hopefully, he will read this book and experience the love and forgiveness of God in his own heart also.

Truly, our heavenly Father is the author and giver of all good things. On 23 December 1976, my wife and I were blessed with the birth of our second child, Chip. Incidentally, both of our sons have committed their lives to Jesus Christ, and Christ is truly their Lord and Savior and King.

Remember, it's not who you are but whose you are. I hope that my time with you has opened your eyes and heart to Jesus Christ, for without Him there is no hope.

On the average, three people die every second in this world, a hundred eighty people die every minute, ten thousand eight hundred die every hour, two hundred fifty-nine thousand of us die every day, and approximately ninety four million people die every year in this world. One year will be your year, one day will be your day, your hour, your minute. Life does not shout, it just runs out sooner than we think.

The message of the Bible is not very complicated. In fact, it's very simple. The message of the Bible is this: The world is a mess, and spiritually speaking, apart from Jesus Christ, I'm a mess, and so are you. We all need a Savior. The name "Jesus" means Savior in Hebrew. He is the hope of this world. The Bible tells us that He went to Calvary's cross, and there on that cross He took your sin and my sin upon Himself. Jesus Christ died for the sins of the world, and the Bible tells us if we believe in Him and accept Him as Lord and Savior and ask Him into our hearts, our sins are forgiven because He paid the penalty for us and we are washed white as snow.

Jesus Christ is alive and He is the only hope in this world.

Does this mean you won't experience any more problems in life? No, the Christian is not exempt from problems, but Jesus tells us to come to Him, all who are weary and burdened and He will give us rest (Matt. 11:28). And, He promises He will never leave or forsake us, for He has come to give us life and to give it abundantly!

Don't run; be still and look up. I know from whence I speak. I ran from Jesus Christ for thirty years. I encourage you to receive the gift of Jesus Christ, and I mean now, right now. This is truly the most important decision you will make in your entire lifetime.

Other Books by Margolyn Woods

Saturday Dads
Grandma's Little Activity Book
Ordinary Women . . . Extraordinary Circumstances

We welcome comments from our readers. Feel free to write to us at the following address:

Editorial Department
Vital Issues Press
P.O. Box 53788
Lafayette, LA 70505

More Good Books from Vital Issues Press

America: Awaiting the Verdict

by Mike Fuselier

We are a nation stricken with an infectious disease. The disease is called betrayal—we are a nation that has denied, rejected, and betrayed our Christian past. The symptoms of the disease are many and multiplying daily. Mike Fuselier, thus, encourages Americans to return to the faith of their founding fathers—the faith upon which our law and government rest—or suffer the consequences. To prove that our forbearers were in no way attempting to establish a secular state, as contended by secular humanists, the author presents oft-forgotten but crucial evidence to fortify his—and all Christians'—case.

ISBN 1-56384-034-0

Anyone Can Homeschool
How to Find What Works for You

by Terry Dorian, Ph.D., and Zan Peters Tyler

Honest, practical, and inspirational, *Anyone Can Homeschool* assesses the latest in homeschool curricula and confirms that there are social as well as academic advantages to home education. Both veteran and novice homeschoolers will gain insight and up-to-date information from this important new book.

ISBN 1-56384-095-2

The Assault: Liberalism's Attack on Religion, Freedom, and Democracy

by Dale A. Berryhill

In *The Liberal Contradiction,* Berryhill showed just how ludicrous it is when civil rights advocates are racists and feminists are sexists. Now he turns to much more disturbing phenomena, revisiting such issues as censorship, civil rights, gay rights and political correctness in education. Fortunately, the American people are catching on to the hypocrisy. Still, the culture war is far from over.

ISBN 1-56384-077-4

Beyond Political Correctness: Are There Limits to This Lunacy?

by David Thibodaux, Ph.D.

Author of the best-selling *Political Correctness: The Cloning of the American Mind,* Dr. David Thibodaux now presents his long awaited sequel—Beyond Political *Correctness: Are There Limits to This Lunacy?* The politically correct movement has now moved beyond college campuses. The movement has succeeded in turning the educational system of this country into a system of indoctrination. Its effect on education was predictable: steadily declining scores on every conceivable test which measures student performance, and, increasing numbers of college freshmen who know a great deal about condoms, homosexuality, and abortion, but whose basic skills in language, math, and science are alarmingly deficient.

ISBN 1-56384-066-9

The Best of HUMAN EVENTS*: Fifty Years of Conservative Thought and Action*

Edited by James C. Roberts

Before Ronald Reagan, before Barry Goldwater, since the closing days of World War II, HUMAN EVENTS stood against the prevailing winds of the liberal political Zeitgeist. HUMAN EVENTS has published the best of three generations of conservative writers—academics, journalists, philosophers, politicians: Frank Chodorov and Richard Weaver, Henry Hazlitt and Hans Sennholz, William F. Buckley and M. Stanton Evans, Jack Kemp and Dan Quayle. A representative sample of their work, marking fifty years of American political and social history, is here collected in a single volume.

ISBN 1-56384-018-9

Can Families Survive in Pagan America?

by Samuel Dresner

Drug addiction, child abuse, divorce, and the welfare state have dealt terrible, pounding blows to the family structure. At the same time, robbery, homicide, and violent assaults have increased at terrifying rates. But, according to the author, we can restore order to our country and our lives. Using the tenets of Jewish family life and faith, Dr. Dresner calls on Americans from every religion and walk of life to band together and make strong, traditional families a personal and national priority again—before it's too late.

ISBN 1-56384-080-4

Conquering the Culture
The Fight for Our Children's Souls

by David Paul Eich

Remember Uncle Screwtape? He was the charming C.S. Lewis character who tried to educate his nephew, Wormwood, on the art of destroying souls. Now, from a fictional town in Montana, comes a similar allegory. This compelling book is a valuable source of support for parents who need both answers and courage to raise moral children in an immoral world.

ISBN 1-56384-101-0

Children No More:
How We Lost a Generation

by Brenda Scott

Child abuse, school yard crime, gangland murders, popular lyrics laced with death motifs, twisted couplings posing as love on MTV and daytime soap operas (both accessible by latch-key children), loving parents portrayed as the enemy, condom pushers, drug apologists, philandering leaders . . . is it any wonder that heroes and role models are passe? The author grieves the loss of a generation but savors a hope that the next can be saved.

ISBN 1-56384-083-9

Combat Ready
How to Fight the Culture War

by Lynn Stanley

The culture war between traditional values and secular humanism is escalating. At stake are our children. The schools, the liberal media, and even the government, through Outcome Based Education, are indoctrinating our children with moral relativism, instead of moral principles. *Combat Ready* not only discloses the extent to which our society has been influenced by this "anything goes" mentality, it offers sound advice about how parents can protect their children and restore our culture to its biblical foundation.

ISBN 1-56384-074-X

Global Bondage: The U.N. Plan to Rule the World

by Cliff Kincaid

The U.N. is now openly laying plans for a World Government—to go along with its already functioning World Army. These plans include global taxation and an International Criminal Court that could prosecute American citizens. In *Global Bondage*, journalist Cliff Kincaid blows the lid off the United Nations. He warns that the move toward global government is gaining ground and that it will succeed if steps are not taken to stop it.

ISBN: Trade Paper 1-56384-103-7
ISBN: Hardcover 1-56384-109-6

One Man, One Woman, One Lifetime: An Argument for Moral Tradition

by Reuven Bulka

Lifestyles that have been recognized since antiquity as destructive and immoral are promoted today as acceptable choices. Rabbi Reuven Bulka challenges the notion that contemporary society has outgrown the need for moral guidelines. Using both scientific research and classical biblical precepts, he examines changing sexual mores and debunks the arguments offered by activists and the liberal media.

ISBN 1-56384-079-0

Getting Out: An Escape Manual for Abused Women

by Kathy L. Cawthon

Four million women are physically assaulted by their husbands, ex-husbands, and boyfriends each year. Of these millions of women, nearly 4,000 die. Kathy Cawthon, herself a former victim of abuse, uses her own experience and the expertise of law enforcement personnel to guide the reader through the process of escaping an abusive relationship. Getting Out also shows readers how they can become whole and healthy individuals instead of victims, giving them hope for a better life in the future.

ISBN: 1-56384-093-6

Handouts and Pickpockets: Our Government Gone Berserk

by William P. Hoar

In his new book, William P. Hoar, a noted political analyst, echoes the sentiments of millions of Americans who are tired of being victimized by their own government. Hoar documents attacks on tradition in areas as diverse as the family and the military and exposes wasteful and oppressive tax programs. This chronicle of our government's pitiful decline into an overgrown Nanny State is shocking, but more shocking is Hoar's finding that this degeneration was no accident.

ISBN 1-56384-102-9

Out of Control—Who's Watching Our Child Protection Agencies?

by Brenda Scott

This book of horror stories is true. The deplorable and unauthorized might of Child Protection Services is capable of reaching into and destroying any home in America. No matter how innocent and happy your family may be, you are one accusation away from disaster. Social workers are allowed to violate constitutional rights and often become judge, jury, and executioner. Innocent parents may appear on computer registers and be branded "child abuser" for life. Every year, it is estimated that over 1 million people are falsely accused of child abuse in this country. You could be next, says author and speaker Brenda Scott.

ISBN 1-56384-080-4

Hidden Dangers of the Rainbow

by Constance Cumbey

The first book to uncover and expose the New Age movement, this national #1 best-seller paved the way for all other books on the subject. This book provides the vivid exposé of the New Age movement, which the author contends is dedicated to wiping out Christianity and establishing a one world order. This movement, a vast network of occult and pagan organizations, meets the tests of prophecy concerning the Antichrist.

ISBN 0-910311-03-X

Political Correctness: The Cloning of the American Mind

by David Thibodaux, Ph.D.

The author, a professor of literature at the University of Southwestern Louisiana, confronts head-on the movement that is now being called Political Correctness. Political correctness, says Thibodaux, "is an umbrella under which advocates of civil rights, gay and lesbian rights, feminism, and environmental causes have gathered." To incur the wrath of these groups, one only has to disagree with them on political, moral, or social issues. To express traditionally Western concepts in universities today can result in not only ostracism, but even suspension. (According to a recent "McNeil-Lehrer News Hour" report, one student was suspended for discussing the reality of the moral law with an avowed homosexual. He was reinstated only after he apologized.)

ISBN 1-56384-026-X

Exposing the AIDS Scandal

by Paul Cameron, M.D.

AIDS is 100 percent fatal all of the time. There are believed to be over 1,500,000 people in the United States carrying the AIDS virus. The ever-growing number of cases compels us to question whether there will be a civilization in twenty years.

ISBN 1-56384-023-5

Inside the New Age Nightmare

by Randall Baer

Are your children safe from the New Age movement? This former New Age leader, one of the world's foremost experts in crystals, brings to light the darkest of the darkness that surrounds the New Age movement. The week that Randall Baer's original book was released, he met with a puzzling and untimely death—his car ran off a mountain pass. His death is still regarded as suspicious.

ISBN 1-56384-022-7

Don't Touch That Dial: The Impact of the Media on Children and the Family

by Barbara Hattemer & Robert Showers

Men and women without any stake in the outcome of the war between the pornographers and our families have come to the qualified, professional agreement that the media does have an effect on our children—an effect that is devastatingly significant. Highly respected researchers, psychologists, and sociologists join the realm of pediatricians, district attorneys, parents, teachers, pastors, and community leaders—who have diligently remained true to the fight against filthy media—in their latest comprehensive critique of the modern media establishment (i.e., film, television, print, art, curriculum).

ISBN Quality Trade Paper 1-56384-032-4
ISBN Hardcover 1-56384-035-9

Kinsey, Sex and Fraud: The Indoctrination of a People

by Dr. Judith A. Reisman and Edward Eichel

Kinsey, Sex and Fraud describes the research of Alfred Kinsey which shaped Western society's beliefs and understanding of the nature of human sexuality. His unchallenged conclusions are taught at every level of education—elementary, high school, and college—and quoted in textbooks as undisputed truth. The authors clearly demonstrate that Kinsey's research involved illegal experimentations on several hundred children. The survey was carried out on a non-representative group of Americans, including disproportionately large numbers of sex offenders, prostitutes, prison inmates, and exhibitionists.

ISBN 0-910311-20-X

The Question of Freemasonry

by Ed Decker

Blood oaths, blasphemy, and illegal activity—in this day and age it's hard to believe these aberrations still exist; this booklet demonstrates that the Freemasons are not simply a "goodwill," community-oriented organization.

ISBN 1-56384-020-0

Delicate Balance

by John Zajac

Find out what forces in the universe are at work and why the earth is in a very delicate balance. The author displays his research to present the overall picture at hand that packages and interconnects economics, prophecy, ecology, militarism, and theology. Can modern science unlock the mysteries of the future? Can we determine our own fate—or are we part of a larger scheme beyond our control?

ISBN 0-910311-57-9

"Soft Porn" Plays Hardball

by Dr. Judith A. Reisman

With amazing clarity, the author demonstrates that pornography imposes on society a view of women and children that encourages violence and sexual abuse. As crimes against women and children increase to alarming proportions, it's of paramount importance that we recognize the cause of this violence. Pornography should be held accountable for the havoc it has wreaked in our homes and our country.

ISBN Trade Paper 0-910311-65-X
ISBN Hardcover 0-910311-92-7

A Call to Manhood: In a Fatherless Society

by David E. Long

Western society is crumbling—from the collapse of the family . . . to our ailing economic system, from the scandals in the church . . . to the corruptions in the Halls of Congress, from the decline of business . . . to the pollution of Hollywood, everywhere, we see moral and societal decay. The reason, says author David Long, is that the vast majority of men in America have received tragically inadequate fathering, ranging from an ineffective father to no father at all. This book presents a refreshing vision and a realistic strategy for men to recapture their biblical masculinity.

ISBN 1-56384-047-2

A Jewish Conservative Looks at Pagan America

by Don Feder

With eloquence and insight that rival essayists of antiquity, Don Feder's pen finds his targets in the enemies of God, family, and American tradition and morality. Deftly . . . delightfully . . . the master allegorist and Titian with a typewriter brings clarity to the most complex sociological issues and invokes giggles and wry smiles from both followers and foes. Feder is Jewish to the core, and he finds in his Judaism no inconsistency with an American Judeo-Christian ethic. Questions of morality plague school administrators, district court judges, senators, congressmen, parents, and employers; they are wrestling for answers in a "changing world." Feder challenges this generation and directs inquirers to the original books of wisdom: the Torah and the Bible.

ISBN Trade Paper 1-56384-036-7
ISBN Hardcover 1-56384-037-5

Trojan Horse— How the New Age Movement Infiltrates the Church

by Samantha Smith & Brenda Scott

New Age/Occult concepts and techniques are being introduced into all major denominations. The revolution is subtle, cumulative, and deadly. Through what door has this heresy entered the church? Authors Samantha Smith and Brenda Scott attempt to demonstrate that Madeleine L'Engle has been and continues to be a major New Age source of entry into the church. Because of her radical departure from traditional Christian theology, Madeleine L'Engle's writings have sparked a wave of controversy across the nation. She has been published and promoted by numerous magazines, including Today's Christian Woman, Christianity Today and others. The deception, unfortunately, has been so successful that otherwise discerning congregations and pastors have fallen into the snare that has been laid.

ISBN 1-56384-040-5

Loyal Opposition: A Christian Response to the Clinton Agenda

by John Eidsmoe

The night before the November 1992 elections, a well-known evangelist claims to have had a dream. In this dream, he says, God told him that Bill Clinton would be elected President, and Christians should support his Presidency. What are we to make of this? Does it follow that, because God **allowed** Clinton to be President; therefore, God **wants** Clinton to be president? Does God **want** everything that God **allows**? Is it possible for an event to occur even though that event displeases God? How do we stand firm in our opposition to the administration's proposals when those proposals contradict biblical values? And how do we organize and work effectively for constructive action to restore our nation to basic values?

ISBN 1-56384-044-8

The Liberal Contradiction

by Dale A. Berryhill

Why are liberals who took part in student demonstrations in the 1960s now trying to stop Operation Rescue from using the very same tactics? Liberalism claims to advocate some definite moral positions: racism and sexism are wrong; tolerance is right; harming the environment is wrong; protecting it is right. But, contemporary liberalism is undermining its own moral foundation. It contends that its positions are morally right and the opposites are wrong, while at the same time, it denies that a moral law (right and wrong) exists. This is the **Liberal Contradiction** and it leads to many ludicrous (and laughable) inconsistencies.

ISBN 1-56384-055-3

En Route to Global Occupation

by Gary Kah

High-ranking government liaison Gary Kah warns that national sovereignty will soon be a thing of the past. Invited to join the WCPA (World Constitution and Parliamentary Association), the author was involved in the planning and implementation of a one-world government. For the skeptical observer, the material in this book "should serve as ample evidence that the drive to create a one-world government is for real." Reproductions of the original documentation are included.

ISBN 0-910311-97-8

God's Rebels

by Henry Lee Curry III

From his unique perspective, Dr. Henry Lee Curry III offers a fascinating look at the lives of some of our greatest Southern religious leaders during the Civil War. The rampant Evangelical Christianity prominent at the outbreak of the Civil War, asserts Dr. Curry, is directly traceable to the 2nd Great Awakening of the early 1800s. The evangelical tradition, with its emphasis on strict morality, individual salvation, and emotional worship, had influenced most of Southern Protestantism by this time. Southerners unquestionably believed the voice of the ministers to be the "voice of God"; consequently, the church became one of the most powerful forces influencing Confederate life and morale. Inclined toward a Calvinistic emphasis on predestination, the South was confident that God would sustain its way of life.

ISBN: Trade Paper 0-910311-67-6
ISBN: Hardcover 0-910311-68-4

Exposing the AIDS Scandal

by Dr. Paul Cameron

Where do you turn when those who control the flow of information in this country withhold the truth? Why is the national media hiding facts from the public? Can AIDS be spread in ways we're not being told? Finally, a book that gives you a total account for the AIDS epidemic, and what steps can be taken to protect yourself. What you don't know can kill you!

ISBN 0-910311-52-8

To Moroni With Love

by Ed Decker

Readers are led through the deepest of the Mormon church doctrines and encouraged to honestly determine whether the words can be construed as heresy. Decker reveals shocking material that has caused countless Mormons to question the church leaders and abandon Mormonism's false teachings.

ISBN 1-56384-021-9

Out of Control—Who's Watching Our Child Protection Agencies?

by Brenda Scott

This book of horror stories is true. The deplorable and unauthorized might of Child Protection Services is capable of reaching into and destroying any home in America. No matter how innocent and happy your family may be, you are one accusation away from disaster. Social workers are allowed to violate constitutional rights and often become judge, jury, and executioner. Innocent parents may appear on computer registers and be branded "child abuser" for life. Every year, it is estimated that over 1 million people are falsely accused of child abuse in this country. You could be next, says author and speaker Brenda Scott.

ISBN 1-56384-069-3

Hitler and the New Age

by Bob Rosio

Hail Caesar! Heil Hitler! Hail—who? Who will be next? Many recognize Caesar and Nero and Hitler as forerunners of the future, when one leader, backed by one government and religious church, will lead one worldwide system. The question is, Were they all tools to prepare the way for the very old and evil world order? Bob Rosio believes that studying an extreme type of historical figure, such as Hitler, will help Christians better understand and better prepare a battle plan to stand against the New Age movement and this emerging world order. He describes this book as "a study in the mechanics of evil."

ISBN 1-56384-009-X

High on Adventure Stories of Good, Clean, Spine-tingling Fun

by Stephen Arrington

From meeting a seventeen-and-a-half-foot great white shark face to face, to diving from an airplane toward the earth's surface at 140 M.P.H., to exploring a sunken battle cruiser from World War II in the dark depths of the South Pacific Ocean, author and adventurer Stephen Arrington retells many exciting tales from his life as a navy frogman and chief diver for the Cousteau Society. Each story is laced with Arrington's Christian belief and outlook that life is an adventure waiting to be had.

ISBN 1-56384-082-0

How to Homeschool (Yes, You!)

SALT SERIES BOOKLET

by Julia Toto

Have you considered homeschooling for your children, but you just don't know where to begin? This book is the answer to your prayer. It will cover topics, such as: what's the best curriculum for your children, where to find the right books, do certified teachers teach better than stay-at-home moms; and what to tell your mother-in-law.

ISBN 1-56384-059-6

The Walking Wounded
A Look at Faith Theology

by Jeremy Reynalds

Is the faith movement saving souls—or destroying lives? After a pastor's wife dies of cancer, he is told that it was due to a lack of faith. A woman in Sweden is so traumatized by the faith movement that she enters a treatment program for ex-cult members to recover. According to a recent study cited by the author, many former faith members appear to have developed severe psychiatric problems from their experiences. Read what he has to say and decide for yourself whether word of faith doctrine is orthodox Christianity or outright heresy.

ISBN 1-56384-076-6

Revival: Its Principles and Personalities

by Winkie Pratney

Are you disturbed by the apathy and despondency of people today? Do you wonder what the future holds for this immoral world? In an age in which values are questioned, families are falling apart, and quality is being replaced by quantity, there is an ever-growing need for a revival of the morals and beliefs of a more stable time. This book is a guide to revival, focusing on past revivals—their personalities and principles—in order to stir all people to seek and expect future revivals.

ISBN 1-56384-058-8

The Burning of a Strange Fire

by Barney Fuller

To over 7 million people, Joseph Smith is the greatest of all prophets. But in *The Burning of a Strange Fire* the reader will witness that Joseph Smith is, perhaps, the greatest false prophet the world has ever seen. Most Mormons have no knowledge of the very powerful occult spirits that provided Joseph Smith with his mysterious prophetic anointing. As a former Mormon elder, Mr. Fuller takes the reader into the early life of the Mormon prophet. He reveals the most successful deception in Christian history.

ISBN 1-56384-049-9

Inside the New Age Nightmare

by Randall Baer

Now, for the first time, one of the most powerful and influential leaders of the New Age movement has come out to expose the deceptions of the organizations he once led. New Age magazines and articles for many years hailed Randall Baer as their most "radically original" and "advanced" thinker . . . "light years ahead of others" says leading New Age magazine *East-West Journal.* His best-selling books on quartz crystals, self-transformation, and planetary ascension have won worldwide acclaim and been extolled by New Agers from all walks of life. Hear, from a New Age insider, the secret plans they have spawned to take over our public, private, and political institutions. Discover the seduction of the demonic forces at work—turned from darkness to light, Randall Baer reveals the methods of the New Age movement as no one else can. Find out what you can do to stop the New Age movement from destroying our way of life.

ISBN 0-910311-58-7

The Parched Soul of America: A Poet's View on Our National Decay

by Leslie Kay Hedger with David Reagan

With breathtaking eloquence and astonishing accuracy, modern-day Isaiah and poet Leslie Kay Hedger demonstrates the stagnancy of America's once-majestic image. Using her pen as a weapon, the poet exposes and attacks the forces undermining our culture: Political decadence; the disintegration of the family; and materialism, hedonism, and religious apostasy. America is a nation in rebellion against God. The writer's heartfelt message: "Turn from your wicked ways and live!"

ISBN 1-56384-031-6

Dinosaurs and the Bible

by David W. Unfred

Every reader, young and old, will be fascinated by this ever-mysterious topic—exactly what happened to the dinosaurs? Author David Unfred draws a very descriptive picture of the history and fate of the dinosaurs, using the Bible as a reference guide. Does the Bible mention dinosaurs? What happened to dinosaurs, or are there some still living, awaiting discovery?

ISBN Hardcover 0-910311-70-6

Please Tell Me— Questions People Ask about Freemasonry . . . and the Answers

by Tom C. McKenney

Since the publication of his first book, *The Deadly Deception*, Tom McKenney has appeared on over 200 talk shows, answering tough questions about Freemasonry from viewers and audiences throughout the USA and Canada. Now, in his latest book, McKenney has compiled the questions most often asked by the public concerning the cult-like nature and anti-Christian activities of the Masonic movement. McKenney tackles topics such as: Masonry's occult roots; Death Oaths and Masonic Execution; Masonry and the Illuminati; and Masonry's opposition to Christian schools. Tom McKenney warns Christians of all denominations to extricate themselves from Masonic movements.

ISBN 1-56384-013-8

How the Government Can Legally Abduct Your Child

SALT SERIES

by Janson A. Kauser

If you don't want to have your child taken away, this might be the most important book you'll ever read. One telephone call from a misguided neighbor or teacher—even a store employee—can launch an investigation by the Department of Social Services. Attorney Janson Kauser explains how to increase your chances of surviving an investigation with your family intact, including what you should—and shouldn't—do at each stage of the process. Real abuse should never be condoned, but no family today is immune from the threat of false accusations.

ISBN: 1-56384-104-5

Parent Police: The U.N. Wants Your Child

SALT SERIES

by Ingrid J. Guzman

Recently, the U.N. General Assembly adopted a treaty that could end parenting as we know it. In a misguided attempt to protect children, the treaty would give them responsibilities that have traditionally belonged to parents. Among other things, it would give a child the right to associate with anyone he chooses (Article 15); to object to all religious training (Article 14); and to see, hear, or read whatever he chooses (Article 13). No one who is truly concerned about the welfare of children can support this treaty.

ISBN: 1-56384-096-5

New World Order: The Ancient Plan of Secret Societies

by William T. Still

For thousands of years, secret societies have cultivated an ancient plan which has powerfully influenced world events. Until now, this secret plan has remained hidden from view. This book presents new evidence that a military take-over of the U.S. was considered by some in the administration of one of our recent presidents. Although averted, the forces behind it remain in secretive positions of power.

ISBN 0-910311-64-1

The Extermination of Christianity–A Tyranny of Consensus

by Paul Schenck with Robert L. Schenck

If you are a Christian, you might be shocked to discover that: Popular music, television, and motion pictures are consistently depicting you as a stooge, a hypocrite, a charlatan, a racist, an anti-Semite, or a con artist; you could be expelled from a public high school for giving Christian literature to a classmate; and you could be arrested and jailed for praying on school grounds. This book is a catalogue of anti-Christian propaganda—a record of persecution before it happens!

ISBN 1-56384-051-0

Goddess Earth— Exposing the Pagan Agenda of the Environmental Movement

by Samantha Smith

There's a new powerhouse in Washington, wielding ominous influence in Congress—it's called the Environmental movement. Its roots are pagan and its agenda is conspicuously anti-Christian. We should be concerned that the recurring theme of Earth Day and Earth Summit was World Government and a New World Order. The Environmental movement, says Samantha Smith, is a very powerful force attempting to implement World Government.

ISBN 1-56384-064-2

The Dark Side of Freemasonry

by Ed Decker

This book is probably the most significant document ever prepared on the subject of the dark side of the Masonic Lodge. In June 1993, a group of Christian researchers, teachers, and ministry leaders met in Knoxville, Tennessee, to gather together all available information on the subject of Freemasonry and its relationship to the Christian world. Ed Decker brought this explosive material back from Knoxville and here presents it as a warning to those who are unaware of the danger of the Masonic movement.

ISBN 1-56384-061-8

Conservative, American & Jewish— I Wouldn't Have It Any Other Way

by Jacob Neusner

Neusner has fought on the front lines of the culture war and here writes reports about sectors of the battles. He has taken a consistent, conservative position in the academy, federal agencies in the humanities and the arts, and in the world of religion in general and Judaism in particular. Engaging, persuasive, controversial in the best sense, these essays set out to change minds and end up touching the hearts and souls of their readers.

ISBN 1-56384-048-0

Subtle Serpent: New Age in the Classroom

by Darylann Whitemarsh & Bill Reisman

There is a new morality being taught to our children in public schools. Without the consent or even awareness of parents—educators and social engineers are aggressively introducing new moral codes to our children. In most instances, these new moral codes contradict traditional values. Darylann Whitemarsh (a 1989 Teacher of the Year recipient) and Bill Reisman (educator and expert on the occult) combine their knowledge to expose the deliberate madness occurring in our public schools.

ISBN 1-56384-016-2

Gays & Guns
The Case against Homosexuals in the Military

by John Eidsmoe

The homosexual revolution seeks to overthrow the Laws of Nature. A Lieutenant Colonel in the United States Air Force Reserve, Dr. John Eidsmoe eloquently contends that admitting gays into the military would weaken the combat effectiveness of our armed forces. This cataclysmic step would also legitimize homosexuality, a lifestyle that most Americans know is wrong.

While echoing Cicero's assertion that "a sense of what is right is common to all mankind," Eidsmoe rationally defends his belief. There are laws that govern the universe, he reminds us. Laws that compel the earth to rotate on its axis, laws that govern the economy; and so there is also a moral law that governs man's nature. The violation of this moral law is physically, emotionally and spiritually destructive. It is destructive to both the individual and to the community of which he is a member.

ISBN Trade Paper 1-56384-043-X
ISBN Hardcover 1-56384-046-4

I Shot an Elephant in My Pajamas— The Morrie Ryskind Story

by Morrie Ryskind with John H. M. Roberts

The Morrie Ryskind story is a classic American success story. The son of Russian Jewish immigrants, Ryskind went on to attend Columbia University and achieve legendary fame on Broadway and in Hollywood, win the Pulitzer Prize, and become a noted nationally syndicated columnist. Writing with his legendary theatrical collaborators George S. Kaufman and George and Ira Gershwin, their political satires had an enormous impact on the development of the musical comedy. In Hollywood, many classic films and four of the Marx Brothers' sublime romps also bear the signatory stamp of genius—Morrie Ryskind.

Forced by his increasingly conservative views to abandon script-writing in Hollywood, Ryskind had the satisfaction near the end of his life to welcome into his home his old friend, the newly elected President of the United States, Ronald Reagan.

ISBN 1-56384-000-6

The Media Hates Conservatives: How It Controls the Flow of Information

by Dale A. Berryhill

Here is clear and powerful evidence that the liberal leaning news media brazenly attempted to influence the outcome of the election between President George Bush and Candidate Bill Clinton. Through a careful analysis of television and newspaper coverage, this book confirms a consistent pattern of liberal bias (even to the point of assisting the Clinton campaign).

The major media outlets have taken sides in the culture war. Through bias, distortion, and the violation of professional standards, they have opposed the traditional values embraced by conservatives and most Americans, to the detriment of our country.

ISBN 1-56384-060-X

New Gods for a New Age

by Richmond Odom

There is a new state religion in this country. The gods of this new religion are Man, Animals, and Earth. Its roots are deeply embedded in Hinduism and other Eastern religions. The author of *New Gods for a New Age* contends that this new religion has become entrenched in our public and political institutions and is being aggressively imposed on all of us.

This humanistic-evolutionary world view has carried great destruction in its path which can be seen in college classrooms where Christianity is belittled, in the courtroom where good is called evil and evil is called good, and in government where the self-interest of those who wield political power is served as opposed to the common good.

ISBN 1-56384-062-6

Homeless in America: The Solution

by Jeremy Reynalds

Author Jeremy Reynald's current shelter, Joy Junction, located in Albuquerque, New Mexico, has become the state's largest homeless shelter. Beginning with fifty dollars in his pocket and a lot of compassion, Jeremy Reynalds now runs a shelter that has a yearly budget of over $600,000. He receives no government or United Way funding. Anyone who desires to help can, says Reynalds. If you feel a burden to help those less fortunate than you, read this book.

ISBN 1-56384-063-4

Delicate Balance

by John Zajac

Find out what forces in the universe are at work and why the earth is in a very delicate balance. The author displays his research to present the overall picture at hand that packages and interconnects economics, prophecy, ecology, militarism, and theology. Can modern science unlock the mysteries of the future? Can we determine our own fate—or are we part of a larger scheme beyond our control?

ISBN 0-910311-57-9

Battle Plan: Equipping the Church for the 90s

by Chris Stanton

Already into the nineties and it's easy to see that the institutions of American society—the family, the church, the government—will continue to look little like the same entities of all prior decades! The evidences have been discussed before. Now is the time to talk about why and what to do about it. A new battle plan is needed. The author dissects the characteristics of the enemy and the effectiveness of its attacks on the church. Then he lays out the military strategy for the spiritual warriors of the 1990s. The enemy won't know what hit him if the Church diligently readies itself for this all-important battle!

ISBN 1-56384-034-0

Journey into Darkness: Nowhere to Land

by Stephen L. Arrington

This story begins on Hawaii's glistening sands and ends in the mysterious deep with the Great White Shark. In between, he found himself trapped in the drug smuggling trade—unwittingly becoming the "Fall Guy" in the highly publicized John Z. DeLorean drug case. Naval career shattered, his youthful innocence tested, and friends and family put to the test of loyalty, Arrington locked on one truth during his savage stay in prison and endeavors to share that critical truth now. Focusing on a single, important message to young people—to stay away from drugs—the author recounts his horrifying prison experience and allows the reader to take a peek at the source of hope and courage that helped him survive.

ISBN 1-56384-003-3

America Betrayed

by Marlin Maddoux

This hard-hitting book exposes the forces in our country that seek to destroy the family, the schools, our culture, and our values. The author details exactly how the news media manipulates your mind. Maddoux is the host of the popular national radio talk show "Point of View."

ISBN 0-910311-18-8

False Security: Has the New Age Given Us a False Hope?

by Jerry Parks

The Great Tribulation! Wars, famine, pestilence, persecution—these are just some of the frightful events in the future of the world. Are they in your future? For centuries, the prophets searched the Scriptures for the timing of the first coming of the Messiah. Now, we watch and wait for the Second Coming of Christ and everything that foreshadows it. In *False Security: Has the New Age Given Us a False Hope?*, author Jerry Parks discusses a relatively recent teaching that has infiltrated the Church, giving many a false hope. When will the Rapture occur? Be prepared to examine your own beliefs and clear up many of the questions you might have about the close of this age.

ISBN 1-56384-012-X

One Year to a College Degree

by Lynette Long & Eileen Hershberger

College—Anyone who's been through the gauntlet of higher education's administrative red tape can attest to the frustration and confusion that accompanies the process. Twenty-eight years after a failed first semester, co-author Eileen Hershberger embarked on the admirable, albeit frightening venture, as an adult learner. One year later she earned her bachelor's degree. With Lynette Long, she reveals the secret in this thorough self-help book, complete with reference guide, work sheets, and resource lists. Most intriguing are the inside tips only professors and upper-level counselors would know.

ISBN 1-56384-001-4

The Devil's Web

by Pat Pulling with Kathy Cawthon

This explosive exposé presents the first comprehensive guide to childhood and adolescent occult involvement. Written by a nationally recognized occult crime expert, the author explains how the violent occult underworld operates and how they stalk and recruit our children, teen-agers, and young adults.

ISBN Trade Paper 0-910311-59-5
ISBN Hardcover 0-910311-63-3

New World Order: The Ancient Plan of Secret Societies

by William T. Still

For thousands of years, secret societies have cultivated an ancient plan that has powerfully influenced world events. Until now, this secret plan has remained hidden from view. This book presents new evidence that a military take-over of the U.S. was considered by some in the administration of one of our recent presidents. Although averted, the forces behind it remain in secretive positions of power.

ISBN 0-910311-64-1

Hidden Dangers of the Rainbow

by Constance Cumbey

The first book to uncover and expose the New Age movement, this national #1 best-seller paved the way for all other books on the subject. It has become a giant in its category. This book provides the vivid exposé of the New Age movement, which the author contends is dedicated to wiping out Christianity and establishing a one world order. This movement, a vast network of occult and pagan organizations, meets the tests of prophecy concerning the Antichrist.

ISBN 0-910311-03-X

When the Wicked Seize a City

by Chuck & Donna McIlhenny with Frank York

A highly publicized lawsuit . . . a house fire-bombed in the night . . . the shatter of windows smashed by politically motivated vandals cuts into the night . . . All because Chuck McIlhenny voiced God's condemnation of a behavior and life-style and protested the destruction of society that results from its practice. That behavior is homosexuality, and that life-style is the gay culture. This book explores: the rise of gay power and what it will mean if Christians do not organize and prepare for the battle, and homosexual attempts to have the American Psychiatric Association remove pedophilia from the list of mental illnesses (now they want homophobia declared a disorder).

ISBN 1-56384-024-3

Teens and Devil Worship

by Charles Evans

Charles Evans was a teen-age Satanist, introduced to the occult through his obsession with heavy metal music. "I noticed that all of my favorite performers promoted occult or satanic practices in their songs . . . Soon I had a personal library in the black arts . . . I easily began leading others into the worship of Satan. Teen-agers would beg to join my coven." His dabbling soon became an addiction. Revealing the whys and hows of teen involvement in Satanism, this book also shows what can be done to prevent involvement.

ISBN 1-56384-004-9

A Jewish Conservative Looks at Pagan America

by Don Feder

With eloquence and insight that rival contemporary commentators and essayists of antiquity, Don Feder's pen finds his targets in the enemies of God, family, and American tradition and morality. Deftly . . . delightfully . . . the master allegorist and Titian with a typewriter brings clarity to the most complex sociological issues and invokes giggles and wry smiles from both followers and foes. Feder is Jewish to the core, and he finds in his Judaism no inconsistency with an American Judeo-Christian ethic. Questions of morality plague school administrators, district court judges, senators, congressmen, parents, and employers; they are wrestling for answers in a "changing world." Feder challenges this generation and directs inquirers to the original books of wisdom: the Torah and the Bible.

ISBN Trade Paper 1-56384-036-7
ISBN Hardcover 1-56384-037-5

Trojan Horse—
How the New Age Movement Infiltrates the Church

by Samantha Smith & Brenda Scott

New Age/Occult concepts and techniques are being introduced into all major denominations. The revolution is subtle, cumulative, and deadly. Through what door has this heresy entered the church? Authors Samantha Smith and Brenda Scott attempt to demonstrate that Madeleine L'Engle has been and continues to be a major New Age source of entry into the church. Because of her radical departure from traditional Christian theology, Madeleine L'Engle's writings have sparked a wave of controversy across the nation. She has been published and promoted by numerous magazines, including *Today's Christian Woman*, *Christianity Today* and others. The deception, unfortunately, has been so successful that otherwise discerning congregations and pastors have fallen into the snare that has been laid.

ISBN 1-56384-040-5

Touching the Face of God

by Bob Russell

This book chronicles the spiritual odyssey of Bob Russell—author, pilot, super-salesman, Christian philosopher. It is the gripping account of one man's love affair with the sky and the obstacles he overcame to become one of America's best-known aviators. It is also the story of how he reaffirmed his faith in everything he did—and how his courage helped him to survive the heartbreaking loss of friends, children, and wife. The author notes his life from the Great Depression until the twilight of the Cold War. It is a true account of survival in the face of poverty and war and an intimate picture of love and marriage.

ISBN Quality Trade Paper 1-56384-010-3
ISBN Hardcover 1-56384-015-4

You Hit Like a Girl

by Elsa Houtz & William J. Ferkile

Rape—it's the issue that dominates the headlines. Have things changed since the days when women and children were afforded respect and care by all members of society? What does self-protection mean in the 1990s in this age of higher rates of violent crime and the "progressiveness" of the women's movement? What can women do to protect themselves? What can men do to protect the women they love—or the children they'd sacrifice their very lives to shelter from harm? The authors, self-defense experts, have developed a thorough guide to self-protection that addresses the mental attitude of common sense safety and details the practical means by which women can protect themselves and their children.

ISBN 1-56384-031-6

Deadly Deception

by Jim Shaw & Tom McKenney

For the first time the 33d degree ritual is made public! Learn of the "secrets" and "deceptions" that are practiced daily around the world. Find out why Freemasonry teaches that it is the true religion, that all other religions are only corrupted and perverted forms of

Freemasonry. If you know anyone in the Masonic movement, you must read this book.

ISBN 0-910311-54-4

Nations without God
The Dawn of Worldwide Government

by Barney Fuller

Those who think of the United Nations as a harmless organization dedicated to the promotion of goodwill need to know the facts. Quietly, the U.N. has infiltrated America and is now in the process of undermining its traditions and values. From the teaching of occultism to schoolchildren, to the requirement that the U.S. military reports its actions to the U.N., Barney Fuller exposes the dangerous trap we are falling into.

ISBN 1-56384-098-7

Hitler and the New Age

by Bob Rosio

Hail Caesar! Heil Hitler! Hail—who? Who will be next? Many recognize Caesar and Nero and Hitler as forerunners of the future, when one leader, backed by one government and religious church, will lead one worldwide system. The question is, Were they all tools to prepare the way for the very old world order? Bob Rosio believes that studying an extreme type of historical figure, such as Hitler, will help Christians better understand and better prepare a battle plan to stand against the New Age movement and this emerging world order. He describes this book as "a study in the mechanics of evil."

ISBN 1-56384-009-X

Hungry for God
Are the Poor Really Unspiritual?

by Larry E. Myers

Inspired by the conviction that the blood of Jesus is the great equalizer, Larry Myers set out to bring much-needed hope and relief to the desperately poor of Mexico. You will be deeply moved by these people, who have so little yet worship their Lord and Savior, even in the midst of their need. You will be inspired by Larry Myers's determination to bring not only medical supplies and food, but light and life to those hungry for God.

ISBN 1056384-075-8

Heresy Hunters:
Character Assassination in the Church

James R. Spencer

An alarming error is sweeping the Christian Church. A small, self-appointed band is confusing Bible-scholarship with character assassination. These *Heresy Hunters* fail to distinguish between genuine error and Christian diversity and turn on their brothers in an ungodly feeding frenzy. Jim Spencer suggests that the heresy hunters themselves might be the real heretics, because their misguided zeal risks splitting the church. He calls upon them to abandon their inquisition.

ISBN 1-56384-042-1

En Route to Global Occupation

by Gary Kah

High-ranking government liaison Gary Kah warns that national sovereignty will soon be a thing of the past. Invited to join the WCPA (World Constitution and Parliamentary Association), the author was involved in the planning and implementation of a one-world government. For the skeptical observer, the material in this book "should serve as ample evidence that the drive to create a one-world government is for real." Reproductions of the original documentation are included.

ISBN 0-910311-97-8

The Basic Steps to Successful Homeschooling

by Vicki A. Brady

If you are a parent already convinced of the moral and intellectual benefits of home education, this book is for you. Working on the premise that home education is a wise decision, Vicki Brady, an expert in the field, provides the reader with a practical, nuts-and-bolts approach to implementing a system of home education. Because of its clear, step-by-step format, this book serves as an invaluable guide for beginner and expert alike in the field of home education. The decision to homeschool is a serious, often intimidating one, but one that serves many families well, if carried out properly. This book will make the decision less daunting, providing home educators with a wealth of knowledge and, therefore, confidence.

ISBN 1-56384-113-4

Order These Huntington House Books !

- *ADD*—
  Theresa Lamson 11.99
- *Alzheimer's*—
  Teresa Strecker, Ph.D. 11.99
- *Anyone Can Homeschool*—
  Terry Dorian & Zan Peters Tyler 10.99
- *Basic Steps to Homeshool*—
  Vicki Brady 11.99
- *Beyond Political Correctness*—
  David Thibodaux 10.99
- *The Big Book*—
  edited by David England 14.99
- *Circle of Death*—
  Richmond Odom 10.99
- *Children No More*—
  Brenda Scott 12.99
- *The Cookbook: Health Begins In Him*—
  Terry Dorian and Rita M. Thomas 14.99
- *The Dark Side of Freemasonry*—
  Ed Decker 10.99
- *Deadly Deception*—
  Shaw\ McKenney 9.99
- *The Demonic Roots of Globalism*—
  Gary Kah 10.99
- *Dinosaurs and the Bible*—
  David Unfred 12.99
  with Teacher's Guide 13.99
- *Do Angels Really Exist?*—
  David O. Dykes 10.99
- *En Route to Global Occupation*—
  Gary Kah 10.99

- *First Lady*—
  Peter and Timothy Flaherty 11.99
- *From Earthquakes To Global Unity*—
  Paul McGuire 10.99
- *Gender Agenda*—
  Dale O'Leary 11.99
- *Getting Out/Abused Women*—
  Kathy Cawthon 10.99
- *Global Bondage*—
  Cliff Kincaid 10.99
- *Global Taxes for World Government*—
  Cliff Kincaid 14.99
- *Handouts and Pickpockets*—
  William P. Hoar 10.99
- *Health Begins in Him*—
  Terry Dorian 10.99
- *Hidden Dangers of the Rainbow*—
  Constance Cumbey 10.99
- *High on Adventure I, II, and III*—
  Stephen Arrington 9.99
- *The Hound of Heaven*—
  Gordon MacDonald 12.99
- *How to be a Great Husband*—
  Tobias Jungreis 11.99
- *How to Homeschool (Yes, You!)*—
  Julia Toto 3.99
- **Inside the New Age Nightmare*—
  Randall Baer 10.99/2.99
- *A Jewish Conservative Looks at Pagan America*—
  Don Feder .... 10.99/21.99 HB
- *Journey into Darkness*—
  Stephen Arrington 10.99